MW00773907

After the Hero's Welcome

A POW Wife's Story
of the Battle Against
a New Enemy

Dorothy Howard McDaniel

95 94 93 92 91   5 4 3 2 1

Library of Congress Catalog Card Number: 91-70344

International Standard Book Number: 0-929387-52-X

Bonus Books, Inc.
160 East Illinois Street
Chicago, Illinois 60611

First Edition

Printed in the United States of America

To those who did not return from Southeast Asia and to those
who'll fly the missions in America's future wars

Contents

Acknowledgments

Many people helped me write this book.

While they were in our home during the writing of their book *Kiss the Boys Goodbye*, Bill Stevenson and Monika Jensen-Stevenson introduced me to the strange world of publishing and encouraged me to tell my story in my own words rather than through those of a "professional." Mary Ann Best and Leslie Genow at the American Defense Institute encouraged me to try and gave generously of their time and energy. Members of the Esther Class in my church gave moral support.

Paul and Marie Miller, Rollie and Vicki Obey, Larry and Judy Bailey, Bob Alotta, Bruce Richards, Stu Johnson, Mary Josiah Howard, Angela Pace, Ruth Gilbert, and Cora Whittington took turns reading the original manuscript, and all of them made valuable suggestions for improving it. John Donovan smoothed out some of the rough places. Leslie Lindsay and John Isaf helped with proofreading. Larry Razbadouski and his editorial staff at Bonus Books were patient with me, a novice at the writing game.

My wonderful children—Mike, Dave, and Leslie—remembered anecdotes that I had forgotten and helped me piece together the story of the hard days we shared while their father was away. Reliving those days with them caused me to look with amazement and gratitude at their resiliency and strength.

Red, my towering six-foot-three husband who stands ten feet tall in my eyes, thought my writing was great even when it wasn't and told me I could do it even when I thought I couldn't. I wanted to write of him and of his commitment to do the right thing no matter what it cost him. *After the Hero's Welcome* is my tribute to Red, my "most admired man" and the love of my life.

1

A New Enemy

The eyes of God move to and fro across the whole earth, seeking a man whose heart is perfect toward Him.

—II Chronicles 16:9

* * *

Could it be that when the eyes of God examine a man, they look for his scars? That the eyes of God look beyond the honors and the accolades, to find the scars?

He had fought his battles. He had paid his dues. At fifty-six it was time to rest, to let others take some hits, to recover from the wounds, to let the scars heal.

But he was fighting the toughest battle of his life. This time, the enemy had no face. He wasn't sure just who the enemy was.

In Hanoi, he knew. Before that, before shoot-down, he knew. Before shoot-down, the enemy was a Soviet-built fighter plane, chasing him through North Vietnamese airspace, hellbent on bagging him. Before shoot-down, the enemy was a surface-to-air missile (SAM), its sophisticated radar device tracking his A-6A Intruder, ready to blow him out of the sky.

Eighty times he had won, somehow managing to evade the MIGs and the SAMs on his combat missions over North Vietnam. He had flown low, circuitous routes, close to the jungle canopy, to throw the MIGs off track. He had learned to "jink" the cumbrous aircraft, jerking it wildly up and down, back and forth, to out-maneuver the radar-guided missiles. On eighty missions, he had jinked the A-6 so many times he now considered himself an expert.

Eighty missions. Almost time to head home, after seven long months of grinding combat. For now, his squadron had flown their share of the missions in America's longest war.

The oddsmakers said you'd get it on your eighty-first. But this one was supposed to be easy. There would be plenty of air cover this time. The Joint Chiefs of Staff had ordered an Alpha strike, a major attack on a primary target. Still, the Air Force was going in first. Just go and get it over with, he thought. I'm ready to go home.

At first, everything seemed okay. Not much flak. No MIGs in sight. Then all hell broke loose. Four SAMs, coming from four directions. He jinked right and left, up and down.

He never saw the fifth SAM. He heard it after it hit. The A-6 pitched down. Bright red warning lights began flashing on and off on the instrument panel, half-obscured by the rising smoke.

"Let's ride it as long as we can, Kelly!" he yelled into the "hot mike" to his bombardier/navigator.

Squinting in the acrid smoke, he spotted a mountain range just ahead, dense tropical foliage covering it almost to the crest. Was it a good place to hide? He knew he had to try to make it to where the search and rescue people could pick them up. He'd wait 'til the very last second.

Now! It had to be now! The plane was going down fast, out of control. Dark green jungle was rushing up to meet them. He ordered Kelly to punch out. He heard the thick plexiglass canopy above his head explode, and braced his body against the hard blast of wind surging into the cockpit as his navigator shot into space. He yanked on his own ejection seat lever and felt the hard jolt that meant he, too, had made it out of the flaming aircraft.

Relieved, he saw that he had a good chute. Floating slowly down through the hot humid air, he watched Kelly's billowing parachute disappear into the tropical trees. He saw his A-6 hit the top of a mountain several miles away and explode into huge pillars of thick black smoke.

He landed in a tall banyan tree, his parachute snagged on a forked limb. Dangling in the air underneath the torn white nylon panels, he could see small figures heading for the foot of the mountain. He knew he had to scramble down and find a place to conceal himself, fast. Groping, he inched his way, hand over hand, up the twisting risers of his chute, trying to grab hold of the trunk of the swaying tree. Hanging on to the rough rope with one hand, he leaned his weight toward the tree trunk and felt the limb holding his parachute peel away. He fell, headlong, fifty feet or so, hitting the ground so hard he could hear the bones in his back crack.

He struggled to get his survival radio out of the zippered pocket of his olive-drab flight suit, hoping to make some kind of contact with Kelly.

"Kelly, do you read? Over."

The black radio crackled with static, but Kelly didn't answer. He tried again, and then again. Nothing.

Forty-five minutes went by before he heard the planes. Then he saw them, "friendlies." They know where I am, he thought, relieved. I'll be out of here by morning.

"I'm on the ground okay," he said into his now damp radio, willing one of the aircraft circling overhead to hear him.

"Roger, Red. See you in the morning."

The raspy voice was familiar. Nick Carpenter, from his own squadron.

It would be a long night. No sensation in his feet and legs, he began to drag himself around on his belly, trying to find Kelly. He told himself it was useless, that Kelly had landed on the opposite side of the mountain. But he knew he had to keep looking. Finally, exhausted, he made a halfhearted attempt to sleep, one ear listening through the darkness, straining to decipher the strange jungle noises. He could hear the distant thrashing sound that had to be machetes, hacking away at the tangled vines.

At dawn, he heard muffled voices coming up the side of the mountain. He was sure they were enemy soldiers, making their way to his hiding place. He searched the empty sky for the rescue planes, the helicopters from Thailand, the Jolly Greens. They're usually pretty reliable, he said to himself. Where are they this morning?

The sun was almost directly overhead when the strange-looking little militiamen burst through the dense green underbrush, AK-47s at the ready. They chattered excitedly about their prize, a downed American pilot, an American "war criminal."

While one of the militiamen trained an AK-47 on him, another one clumsily fashioned a blindfold from a piece of brown ragged burlap, and the tallest of the four men tied it roughly and firmly around his throbbing head, obscuring his vision. He struggled to get to his feet, but two of the soldiers grabbed him and held him while the third one bound his feet with heavy hemp rope, which cut into the flesh just above his ankles. They drew his hands up behind his shoulders until he thought his arms would leave their sockets and then pulled the rough ropes taut, leaving his hands dangling just below his shoulder blades. They dragged his aching body through the underbrush and threw him into the back of a rusty, dilapidated truck. An overpowering smell of gasoline made him nauseous and he thought he was going to pass out.

He was probably on his way to the infamous Hoa Lo Prison in Hanoi, which he guessed would be about fifty miles away. Pilots had dubbed the old French prison that already held many of their fellow aviators the "Hanoi Hilton."

His blindfold had begun to slip slightly and from one corner he could see that two of the angry-looking militiamen had gotten into the back of the truck with him. Then he realized that the smell of gasoline was coming from two, large, open drums, one on each side of him. The gasoline sloshed out on him as the rusty old truck lurched to a start and began the long torturous ride over the deeply-rutted roads to Hanoi.

I hope no one strikes a match, he thought incongruously. I guess that's the least of my worries, he said to himself wryly. He tried to concentrate, to think ahead, to brace himself for what he knew was coming.

I'm going to need all the strength I can muster. Oh, God, I need strength—and I need courage, too—the courage to resist, to hold fast, to not give in.

Every time the old truck hit a bump in the road, he bit his lip to keep from crying out as incredible sharp pain shot through his back. He tried to shift more weight onto his side, but his sudden movement drew a sharp kick in the stomach from the soldier sitting at his head. This time he did cry out in pain and his captor crammed a piece of the burlap into his mouth. He thought he would choke.

Suddenly, in the distance, he could hear what sounded like a very boisterous crowd, chanting some kind of slogan in the strange tongue that he already knew was Vietnamese. The truck slowed, creeping to a stop as the chants grew louder. The soldiers beside him pushed him to the ground and jerked off his blindfold, turning him to face an angry mob of civilians wielding clubs, sticks, and jagged rocks. Some of them began pummeling him with their crude weapons while others cheered wildly.

They're going to let these people kill me, he thought hysterically. They're angry about the bombing attacks, and they need someone to take it out on. I'm going to die here, with my hands and feet bound like an animal in a slaughterhouse. He'd heard that the Vietnamese hated all Americans, especially the tall ones, and for the first time in his life he wished he weren't six feet, three inches tall.

The attack stopped, just as suddenly as it had begun.

They turn these people on and off like a radio, he realized with a shock. They don't want me to die; they want me to suffer. Dying would probably be easier than what's coming, but dying's not an option. But knowing they would keep him alive was *something*, anyway.

They blindfolded him again, this time so he could see nothing, and the painful ride continued. His torn flight suit was now soaked with sweat and gasoline. Then he heard a heavy gate swing open, ancient hinges creaking loudly—and, finally, the clang of the gate slamming behind him.

This has to be Hoa Lo, the old French prison, he thought numbly. We're home. It was almost a relief.

They half-dragged him down a long concrete corridor and heaved his stinking, sore body onto the floor of a dank, musty cell. He heard the lock turn on the other side of the heavy metal door. He lay in a crumpled heap on the gray concrete floor, alone.

In Hanoi, he knew who the enemy was. The enemy had many faces. The enemy was the Vietnamese guard, the "turnkey," the soldier in the sun-bleached khaki fatigues who jangled the key to his cell before unlocking the door and dragging his beat-up body across the rough, jagged concrete to the torture room. The enemy was the stony-faced interrogator who loomed over him, badgering him for a confession of his "war crimes," his "crimes against humanity." The enemy was the sadistic-eyed henchman hoisting the long strip of thick black rubber in his clenched fist, ready to hit him again—and then again—when he refused to "cooperate," to say the words they wanted to hear: that he was the "blackest of criminals."

And the worst enemy was time, the boredom in his solitary cell, the wondering when, and if, he would see his family again.

He came home to a hero's welcome. Through sheer tenacity, and the grace of God, he was able to endure the torture and the isolation for six long, hard years—2,110 days and nights of painful uncertainty.

His country decorated him with the Navy's highest award for bravery, the Navy Cross. And he, in turn, continued to serve the country he had come to love so much.

He savored his freedom. At long last, he could sleep the night through, with no jangling keys to disturb his dreams. He could walk up to a door, any door, turn the knob, and, miraculously, the door would open. He could stand in the shower stall as long as he liked, the blessed hot streams of water balm to his battered body.

He could load his three children, now almost grown, into the yellow station wagon and take them fishing, or to church, or to see a baseball game, or anywhere he liked. He could talk to them, and listen to them, and try to fill in the gap carved by seven years of his absence.

He could put his arms around me again, and brush away my tears with gentle fingers, fingers now numb and stiff from the ropes drawn too tight and left too long on his wrists.

Perhaps he could even fly again, and pick up the pieces of his interrupted Navy career. He wanted to serve his country again, in any way he was needed. He was determined to make his beloved country stronger—and better, if he could.

His joy in being a free man was tempered by knowing that Kelly did not come home with him. He tried to find out what had happened to Kelly after he was downed, but the Vietnamese always answered his questions by saying they knew nothing of his navigator. He believed U.S. officials when they assured him that all the other POWs had come home when he did. And so, he finally accepted Kelly's death and tried to help Kelly's family accept it too.

He wanted to get on with his life, to recoup whatever he could of the six years he had missed, and then go forward. He wouldn't look back.

He was back in the Navy's mainstream before long, and left active duty a man of some stature by virtue of his career experiences. He used his considerable influence to combat the public apathy he believed was causing the United States to become a second-rate power on the world scene. And he relished every opportunity that came his way to alert people to the danger of taking freedom for granted. He had come to consider freedom life's most precious gift.

It never occurred to him that Kelly and some of the other men who had ejected from their crippled aircraft into the jungles of Southeast Asia might still be in captivity. If he had ever really thought about it, he would have been certain that his country would never knowingly leave a serviceman behind after a battle.

The first inkling that some of the missing men might still be alive came during his last tour of duty in the Navy. As Director of Navy/Marine Corps Liaison on Capitol Hill, he was privy to high-level Pentagon briefings on the fate of the men still missing in Southeast Asia. It was in one such briefing that he saw a photograph, taken over Laos by an orbiting intelligence-gathering satellite, of a primitive jungle prison camp. Tall figures—Americans?—were clearly visible in an inner compound of the prison. In another briefing, he learned that the Pentagon was looking into reports from boat people fleeing Indochina that they

had seen Americans in captivity. The intelligence experts called
the reports "live sightings."

He tried to put the photograph and the live sighting reports
out of his mind, telling himself that those charged with the task of
sorting out intelligence gathered in Southeast Asia were compe-
tent and trustworthy, that those in power would leave no stone
unturned to rescue any POWs determined to be still alive. After
all, this was America, and America could not do otherwise.

It wasn't his responsibility to do something about the possibility that POWs were still held in Southeast Asia. He had other
things to do. He retired from the Navy and entered politics. After
an ill-fated congressional campaign, he founded a non-partisan defense organization in Washington, close to the Capitol, so he
could continue to do what he believed needed to be done to keep
his beloved country strong and free.

After the American Defense Institute, which he headed, became highly visible, an underground network of POW family
members, Vietnam veterans, and other POW activists flocked to
his office. They bore hair-raising tales of callous treatment of information about their friends and loved ones still in captivity. Disen-
chanted with what they saw as bureaucratic indifference to the
POW question, they looked to him for leadership in Washington.

But it was the armed forces' lack of trust in their leaders that
bothered him most. The Institute was sponsoring a program encouraging military personnel to register and vote, and it soon became apparent to him that most of the soldiers and sailors he
encountered believed that American POWs had been abandoned
in Southeast Asia by their country.

How can a man go into battle knowing he may be left behind
if he falls? he wondered. *The one thing that kept me going from one
day to the next when I was a POW was knowing that my country would
not let me down, that some day they'd come to get me.*

He knew he had to start asking some hard questions of the
very people whose causes he supported. He knew he had to do everything he could to right what he saw as a terrible wrong.

What he couldn't know was that this would be the toughest
battle of his life. He would go into battle against a new enemy, an
enemy that had no face, an enemy lurking behind closed doors

and hiding in sealed filing cabinets. He would fight an enemy who was supposed to be a friend, who used the coward's weapons of innuendo and outright slander, aimed at destroying his reputation and raising questions about his integrity.

"I have some scars that don't show," Red told me when he came home after six years in a communist prison in Vietnam. Neither of us would have believed that he would bear still more scars, and that these wounds would be inflicted by a faceless enemy in his own country.

2

Navy Wife, Come What May

When I stood at the altar in June of 1956, beside my big, strong Navy pilot with flaming red hair, he promised to love, cherish, and protect me. He should have added, "And I promise you'll never be bored!"

I grew up in Buies Creek, North Carolina, a small college town where my dad was pastor of the local church and professor of Bible at the college. I met Red McDaniel the night he arrived to attend college on a baseball scholarship, and I was instantly attracted to this tall, gangly red-haired athlete from a tobacco farm near Kinston, about eighty miles away. His father was a tenant farmer who loved athletics and had encouraged Red to participate in every sport Grainger High School offered. Red told me his dad had allowed him to choose between "plowing" or "playing."

"Of course, I chose playing to get out of plowing," he laughed.

Red was the oldest of eight children. There was barely enough money to feed and clothe the family so Red had pretty much made his own way since the age of fourteen. His high school athletic coach, Frank Mock, had arranged for Red to get a scholarship at Campbell Junior College and (we found out years later, after Coach Mock's death) had anonymously paid some of his college expenses.

Baseball was Red's love—and his livelihood. Not only did he get baseball scholarships to Campbell and, later, to Elon College, but in the summertime he played semi-pro baseball in the Tobacco

Belt League. The farmers from rural eastern North Carolina would gather on Saturday nights to watch the games. When a player hit a home run or drove in the winning run or did anything else spectacular, they passed their straw hats and baseball caps to collect a reward for the player.

"That's quite an incentive to hit home runs," Red told me, laughing, and he often won the hatfuls of money.

I was the oldest of four and, as the daughter of a preacher, I also knew how it felt to pinch pennies. But my childhood was rich in the ways that count. Our house was full of love and warmth and interesting people, most of them college students my parents were helping in one way or another. One of my favorite stories growing up was how my dad saved enough money to buy my mother a small diamond engagement ring, only to lend all the money to a promising young student to use for college expenses. The story later appeared in *Reader's Digest* and was entitled, "Riches No Diamond Can Buy."

Red and I both graduated from Campbell and then went on to senior colleges, he to Elon College, on a baseball scholarship, of course, and I to the University of North Carolina at Greensboro, where I majored in English.

After graduation, with the draft staring him in the face, Red decided to enter Navy flight training rather than be a foot soldier. He was able to get a temporary coaching/teaching position in a local high school so that when his five-year Navy tour ended, he could fulfill his lifelong ambition to be a baseball coach. He could take advantage of the five-year tenure agreement the state of North Carolina had with public school teachers whose careers were interrupted by military service.

Finally, after Red finished the first stage of flight training at Naval Air Station Pensacola (Florida) and received his ensign's commission, we could afford to get married.

Our honeymoon was a trip to Corpus Christi, Texas, where Red would complete advanced flight training and put on his shiny gold Navy wings.

All my life I had wanted to see New Orleans. As we made our way to Corpus Christi, Red told me we'd probably have time to go the hundred or so miles out of our way and spend a night in the

French Quarter, find a place that served Creole food, and hear some good Dixieland jazz.

The detour point was Biloxi, Mississippi, where we stopped to gas up.

"We can make Corpus some time tomorrow if we drive on to Baton Rouge tonight," Red said as he slid back into the driver's seat.

"What about New Orleans?" I wanted to cry.

"I'd like to head on down to Corpus tonight," he answered. "I need to pick up my orders and find out which of the three auxiliary fields they're assigning me to."

I looked at him. *Maybe we're out of money*, I thought. *Well, Corpus Christi isn't far from New Orleans. We can always drive up for a weekend.* I was a new bride. I decided we weren't going to have our first argument over a one-night visit to New Orleans.

I should have known; his love affair with flying had already begun. He couldn't wait to get back into the cockpit.

Corpus Christi was more like Florida than my idea of Texas. Sprawling along the Gulf Coast, tall palm trees lining the streets, it was a beautiful spot to begin married life. When we arrived, Red wasn't able to get his new assignment early after all so we rented a little cottage by the water's edge and had an extended honeymoon. The cottage had its own pier that jutted out into the Gulf and was ideal for catching the Spanish mackerel and sea trout that were so plentiful in the Gulf of Mexico. Before long, all of Red's bachelor friends had heard about our private fishing spot and they descended upon us in hordes, always managing to stay for dinner. I had never cooked a fish before, but I learned to cook all kinds of fish that week.

"Don't you have any married friends? Or at least some with girlfriends?" I asked Red. But he said most of the guys were still bachelors and hadn't been in Corpus long enough to meet the local girls. When the week ended, however, and Red started flying again, we did meet some of the married couples. We had a lot of parties in the little furnished apartment we rented after our week by the shore ended. It was a whole new world for me. It was fun, and I didn't want to leave our new home when the three months of advanced flight training were over.

But I wasn't sure Navy life was for me. I was already looking forward to the day when flying and military life would end for us and we could go home to North Carolina and live like "normal people." Everything about the Navy was foreign to me, and I didn't like it very much. I was a long way from home, and flying was the only topic of conversation. At parties, the women ended up on one side of the room, the men on the other. We couldn't hear what they were saying, but we knew our student-pilot husbands were rehashing their "hops" by the way their hands glided back and forth through the air, describing the flight patterns they had flown that day.

Well, I can stand anything for five years, I told myself. *Then we'll say goodbye to suitcases and furnished apartments and settle down in our own cozy house somewhere. Our children will grow up in a friendly little town just as we did. Perhaps Red will have winning teams, and a small college somewhere will give him a coaching job. A familiar college town will suit me just fine.*

But for now, I'll try to enjoy the travel and the people we'll meet in our nomadic Navy life. I'll just make the best of it.

I was so proud of Red the day I pinned his new gold aviator's wings on his chest, with the Navy brass and all the other newly-designated naval aviators looking on. He was taller than the others, standing rigidly at attention in his crisp blue Navy uniform with the shiny four-month-old ensign's stripe. My heart was bursting with love for him.

And I was excited about Red's orders. We were going to Virginia Beach, only four hours from my parents' home. We could start our family. The children we wanted to have could get to know their grandparents even before Red left the Navy and went back to his coaching career. And maybe we could stop in New Orleans on our way to Virginia. We had plenty of time.

But this time Red was *really* in a hurry. He was eager to check into his first real squadron and get his fingers on the stick of the A-1 Skyraider he would be flying for the next four years. We drove straight through, taking turns at the wheel, and made it to Virginia Beach three days before Red had to report to Attack Squadron 25 at Naval Air Station Oceana.

Good, I thought. *We'll have time to look for an apartment—and to rest up.*

"I'll go ahead and check in tonight," Red told me just as I spotted the city limit sign. "I can save the rest of my leave for Christmas."

He can't wait to get into that plane, I thought. *Flying's in his blood.*

We moved into a tiny furnished apartment just a block away from the ocean. I studied every service etiquette and protocol book I could get my hands on and threw myself into the many social activities of the squadron wives, determined to fit into the role of Navy wife—for the time being, anyway. Even though we arrived in Virginia Beach after the school year had started, the teacher shortage meant I was able to find a teaching job right away.

I'll be the one who keeps us in touch with the teaching field until we can finish our Navy tour, I thought.

I loved living near the ocean. At night after dinner we'd walk arm in arm along the shore, watching the sea gulls circle overhead and the sun's last rays fleck the foaming waves with gold. I'd put flying out of my mind then, and know that my big, strong aviator would always love me and take care of me, no matter what. And I knew my love for him would survive any hardship Navy life could ever pose for us.

We were expecting our first baby by the time Squadron VA-25 left for their first deployment—a three-month exercise in the North Atlantic. Red and I wanted to save some money to buy our own furniture, so we gave up our little furnished apartment by the ocean, and I went home to spend the three months with my parents in North Carolina.

Very pregnant, I was helping my mother serve tea to the women in her garden club, when one of our small-town, life-long friends asked me very politely, "Will your husband be home when your baby comes?"

I explained to her that, yes, Red would surely be back in time to drive me to the hospital.

"Well, how much longer will it be before he can get *out?*" she asked, her eyebrows rising. I imagined she said it as though Red were in jail or something. After all, nobody from my home town *ever* made a *career* of military service. That is, unless he was incapable of doing anything else.

"He may decide to stay *in*," I heard myself say.

"Oh, I see." And she turned away.

Now, where did that come from, I asked myself. *Red and I haven't even talked about that. But I'm proud of what he does!* Deep inside, I knew he was a naval aviator, through and through. And I was a Navy wife, come what may.

But, then, I didn't know what was coming.

3

The "Poor Me" Days

Vietnam. It looked so small and insignificant on the big world map hanging above the bookcase in our family room. Red hung the map there as soon as the children were old enough to show some interest in his Navy travels. Black dotted lines zigzagged across the continents and the oceans, tracking flights and ship movements that had taken my Navy pilot literally from one corner of the map to the other.

But I had never noticed that tiny sliver of land jutting out into the South China Sea on the other side of the world.

Now, in 1965, most evenings at news time, the commentators talked about mounting U.S. casualties in what was not even a war, not yet anyway. A police action, they called it, in Vietnam.

Navy flyers, mostly from squadrons stationed on the West Coast, were flying sorties over North Vietnam. Antiaircraft guns and radar-guided missiles occasionally found their targets and brought down a few of the fighter-bombers, their pilots killed or captured or, in most cases, simply "missing in action."

Slowly it was coming closer to home. Some Navy fighter squadrons from the East Coast were now being deployed to Southeast Asia, and at least one squadron from NAS Oceana had returned without two of its flyers. Commander Jerry Denton and his navigator Bill Tschudy had been shot down and taken prisoner in North Vietnam. I remembered meeting Jerry and his wife

Jane at a party a couple of years before. I never heard much about Jerry's being a POW, and I had somehow gotten the feeling that it was something you weren't supposed to talk about.

But, one night in May of 1966, Red came bounding in the front door and went straight to the television, ignoring me as I stood at the stove stirring a pot of beef stew.

"Jerry Denton's gonna be on TV," he called to me through the open doorway to the kitchen. "They hauled him out to a press conference in Hanoi. ABC is supposed to carry it tonight."

I turned off the burner under the stew and joined him in front of the TV, my heart in my throat. They were showing Jerry Denton as a prisoner of war? How would he look? What would he say? How did it feel to be Jane right now, waiting to see him on national TV when she hadn't seen him for so long?

Haggard, sitting tensely on the edge of his chair, hands clenched in tight fists, a man we hardly recognized as Jerry Denton blinked his eyes repeatedly in the harsh glare of the camera lights.* His voice was hoarse and gravelly as he spoke of loyalty to his government's policy in Vietnam.

I gasped.

"He looks *terrible!*" The words came slowly.

"I think he looks pretty good," Red commented. "He looks pretty darned good considering what he's been through."

A shiver ran down my spine.

Red hadn't said much about it, but we both knew his turn was coming. He had completed "survival school" in the heavily wooded areas around Brunswick, Maine, learning first how to evade capture and then how to cope with being a prisoner of war. He would, I realized, have a pretty good idea of what Jerry had been going through. The Navy was preparing Red to fly the combat missions, but, if he knew when Attack Squadron 35 would deploy, he hadn't told me. I had just been trying not to think about it. Three active youngsters and a busy Navy social life didn't leave much time for thinking about what could happen tomorrow. Anyway, being married to Red was teaching me not to worry about

---

*Years later, we learned that Jerry had been blinking in Morse code, sending a message about his torture, which U.S. intelligence experts were able to decipher.

what might or might not happen in the future. Every time I would start to worry he would say, "Honey, worrying's like living through it twice."

Red believed in living each day as it came.

In the ten years since I'd pinned on Red's Navy wings, he had circled the globe several times. But his squadrons and ships had all been stationed in the Virginia Beach/Norfolk area.

When his tour with VA-25 at NAS Oceana had ended, he was assigned to VA-42 as a flight instructor, training new pilots to fly the A-1 Skyraider. Then we went to Brunswick, Georgia, for a brief five-month stay while Red underwent training at the Carrier Air Approach Control Center before returning to Norfolk for his tour aboard USS *Independence*. When the Navy adopted the A-6A Intruder, Red was excited about the chance to make the transition from the propeller-driven Skyraider to the Navy's sophisticated new all-weather jet bomber. After the necessary training in VA-42, he was assigned to Oceana's VA-35.

We had outgrown the little house in Virginia Beach we'd purchased when Mike was a baby, and we had carefully selected a building site and planned our own house. It was a perfect home for our growing family. Mike, just finishing second grade, could walk to school, and David could walk with him when he entered first grade in September.

I was still settling into our new home in the Alanton subdivision of Virginia Beach, making curtains for the children's rooms and refinishing some secondhand furniture I had found for Leslie, who had outgrown her crib. Mike and David had their own rooms now, in our pretty new house under the stately pine trees that whispered in the balmy spring nights. Roaring fires in the first fireplace we'd ever had gave a rosy glow to the winter evenings when the pines bent low in the blustery winds.

I had given up my teaching career when David was born, thankful that we could manage on Red's Navy pay. I wanted to stay home with the children while they were preschoolers. But I looked forward to getting back into teaching when the children were older. I loved teaching high school seniors how to write and to appreciate good literature. My child psychology and education courses, however, had taught me how important those first years were in child development, and I was determined to do a good job with our three youngsters. Having Red away much of the time made it doubly important, I thought, since there were times that I had to try to take his place in the family. Besides, I loved all the activities—Cub Scouts, PTA, birthday parties, and just playing with the kids.

Red had applied for a "regular" naval officer's commission just before his mandatory five years of service were up. He had asked me what I wanted him to do, but only because he thought he should. I hadn't had the heart to say, "I want you to get out."

I knew how much he loved flying, and I had learned to accept Navy life, gracefully, I hoped. Each downside had an upside. We had a lot of separations: six-month deployments to the Mediterranean, then six months at home; three-month trips to Guantánamo Bay, Cuba, then three months at home. But we also had a lot of joyful reunions. We lived in a lot of different apartments and houses. But we never got tired of where we lived. We said a lot of goodbyes to friends just as we were getting to know them. On the other hand, we met a lot of new, interesting people.

Red wasn't a full-time father. He wasn't home every night at five o'clock like all the other dads in the neighborhood. But, when he *was* home, he worked hard at having quality time with Mike, David, and Leslie. He worked at it harder than the dads who hurried home each night to catch the evening news, and it showed in his relationships with the children. When he *could* come home at a normal hour, Red rushed out to play catch in the back yard, or to sit on the front steps to listen to the details of his child's day, knowing that another deployment would soon take him away again. He'd taken his share of the child development courses, too, and he wanted to establish good rapport with the children while they were small.

All three of our children were born in between Red's deployments, and he forged a strong bond with each one while they were still babies. When he was at sea, we exchanged tapes back and forth across the oceans so Mike, David, and Leslie wouldn't forget the sound of his voice.

I was determined to make our life together work. Embedded deep in my consciousness were principles planted by the important people of my childhood.

"You do what you have to do," my grandmother said.

"You'll never be happy if you base your life on your feelings," my dad taught me.

And, when I was older, I heard a minister say, "Love is not just a feeling; love is a commitment."

Some of the words may have been trite. But the underlying philosophy and the lives of the people who said the words had somehow connected inside of me, giving me the determination I needed to adapt to the ups and downs of our lives.

When you don't feel like loving, you decide to love. As the mother of three active youngsters, I could see how that applied to my feelings toward my children, especially when they misbehaved. I decided the same principle applied to marriage—and maybe even to the Navy. So far it had worked for me.

And underlying all the homespun philosophy was a deep, abiding faith in God. I had a very personal relationship with Him, relying on Him to provide the strength to live out the philosophy.

It wasn't always easy. For one thing, I didn't like being alone. Some of the cold winter nights when the squadron was at sea seemed to last forever. At least once, I thought I heard someone trying to get in the house through the side door. I sat on the floor 'til dawn, one ear glued to the door, practicing dialing the number of the police in the dark.

But I paid dearly for it the next day. Groggy from my all-night vigil, I wandered around in a stupor, hearing myself snap at the children for the slightest annoyance.

I fell into bed that night, too tired to care *who* broke into the house. I decided that Red was right. Worrying *was* like living through it twice. My grandmother called it borrowing trouble. I knew I wouldn't "borrow trouble" again by hearing imaginary intruders in the night.

Then there were the "poor me" days when I was just plain lonely. I'd get a letter from Red telling me about a sightseeing trip or, worse, a postcard from some exotic Mediterranean port. And I'd think, he has all the fun in this family while I stay home and take care of the kids. I conveniently ignored the fact that Red was putting in some long hard hours on the flight deck, flying fourteen and fifteen-hour hops in his A-1 Skyraider when he wasn't making a rare visit to a foreign port.

The nights were even lonelier when one of the children was restless with a fever or coming down with a cold, and there was no one there to worry with me. The house would seem especially empty on those nights and made the poor me days worse.

I didn't like being an on-again, off-again single parent. I knew it would get more confusing to the children as they got older. We'd become accustomed to our routines, with Mike, David, and Leslie looking to their dad for answers and discipline. Then Dad would leave and I would have to fill that role. No sooner would we establish this new routine, when Red would come home and we'd start all over again. I hadn't learned how to deal with that kind of see-saw parenting in my child psychology courses, and I was concerned about the long-term effect it might have on the children.

But gradually I was learning to cope, to accept the realities of our lives, to live my life as it was instead of how I wished it would be. For one thing, as the children grew, I could see how my frame of mind directly affected their attitudes. When I was cheerful, they were cheerful. When I worried, they worried. That I was directly responsible for the mental state of the children was a heavy burden, but it was a fact of life.

I came to realize I was wishing half my life away. For the six months Red was away, I counted the days until he was home again for six months. When he was home, I dreaded the time he'd leave again. Life was a gift, each day too precious to wish away.

So I learned to make a concerted effort to live one day at a time, to make each day count. Whether or not it was the best of days, I stopped saying "poor me" and tallied up the good things in my life. Counting your blessings, my minister called it. I had always welcomed a challenge. When I finally took a good long look and saw what a challenge life as a Navy wife could be, the poor me days were over.

God was preparing me, little by little, for what only He knew lay ahead.

4

Vietnam: Our Turn

O ur turn in Vietnam came too soon.
      Early in the summer of 1966, I noticed Red was
spending more and more time with Mike, David, and Leslie. He
played catch with the boys in the back yard long after sunset, then
they'd catch fireflies and sit on the porch playing "I Spy" and making up preposterous stories. I noticed he was unusually willing to
postpone Leslie's bedtime for the requested "one more story."

Sitting on the steps watching them, I knew the children would
miss him more than ever this time. *He's thinking about the separation coming up this fall,* I thought. *He's storing up "quality time" with
the children, making sure they have a lot of good things to remember
about him while he's gone.*

VA-35 was scheduled to fly their A-6A Intruders from NAS
Oceana to the West Coast in October to board USS *Enterprise.*
The ship would sail from San Francisco around the first of Novem-
ber and arrive on Yankee Station in the Gulf of Tonkin before
Thanksgiving.

In August we rented a camping rig from Navy Special Services
and drove to the Blue Ridge Mountains. We were taking the two-
week camping trip we had planned to make with the children
when they were a little older. I was concerned that Leslie, at three,
was too little to rough it, but Mike and David were so excited by
the idea that I relented.

"It's a great way to really get away," Red said. "No phones, no mail. Just woods and streams."

Red was right. Both of us had been more than a little tense since learning when the squadron would leave for Vietnam, and Red had been working long hours preparing for deployment. The camping trip was just what we needed. Perhaps we could even build enough memories to last until next summer.

The children would surely never forget our encounter with the grizzly bear.

This brave king of the mountain came lumbering into our campsite around midnight and began helping himself to the contents of our food cooler. The five of us were roused from a sound sleep by the bear's banging on the cooler's hinged lid, which we were sure we had fastened securely. We peeked out of the tent, and there he was, not five feet away.

Red grabbed the baseball bat lying beside the tent opening and started out after the grizzly.

"Red, get back in this tent!" I screeched.

Startled, the bear ran off into the woods.

We never knew whether the baseball bat or my screech scared the bear away, but the children thought it was hilarious that I kept Red from going out to protect the family.

Every night for those two weeks, Red and the boys built a roaring campfire from the wood they gathered during the day. After we finished dinner, we settled down in our sleeping bags to talk and sing and watch the fire burn down. The last night, Red decided to explain to the children where he would be going in October.

"Where's Vietnam?" Mike asked.

"I'll show you on the map when we get home," Red answered. "The important thing is that you know it's a war."

"Are you fighting the Japs or the Germans?" David wanted to know. He and Mike knew all about the fighting in World War II from the war movies they had seen on TV.

"Neither one." Red told him. "It's the Communists in Vietnam this time."

"I thought the Nazis were the bad guys," Mike said.

"Well, it's kind of the same thing," Red explained. "It's about freedom. It's about keeping the bad guys from trying to take over the good guys. Or to take over the guys who can't defend themselves. It's about the bad guys bullying other people."

"And it's my job," he added. "I want you to be brave. And take care of Mommy for me, Mike."

"Okay, Dad." Mike gazed steadily at Red.

"I wish you didn't have to go." David moved closer to Red's knee.

"Me, too, Dave. But I do. It's my job." Red put his arm around Dave's shoulders.

"Are you scared, Daddy?" Mike wanted to know.

"Sure, a little bit. But I'll be okay," Red assured him.

Leslie had fallen asleep. It was getting chilly and I got up to put her in the tent.

"Mommy, are you scared?" David asked me.

"Yeah, I guess, a little. But not as scared as I was when the grizzly bear came in to the camp," I said.

The two boys giggled, and I could hear them recounting the story of the bear to Red's laughter as I carried Leslie into the tent and tucked the covers around her.

When I came back to the campfire, they were telling "knock, knock" jokes. Red's eyes met mine over Dave's head. Don't borrow trouble, his eyes said to me.

But my heart just wasn't in the campfire banter anymore. *Yes, I'm scared*, I thought. *Just how long will my determination and resolve last this winter when you're flying combat missions over North Vietnam? I'm not sure I can handle that.*

"Okay, guys, bedtime." Red got to his feet and started dousing the fire. The boys and I began rolling up the sleeping bags to move them into the tent.

"Look at the stars," I said. "There must be a million of them out tonight."

"Are there more stars in the mountains?" David wanted to know.

"It's the same sky," Mike said. "It just looks like more because we're closer to them."

"Or perhaps because the air is clearer," I said, thankful for the diversion.

The fire out, Red checked the latch on the food cooler in case the grizzly visited the camp again, and we all crawled into our sleeping bags in the tent. Mike and Dave were asleep instantly, and Red and I lay there, holding each other close. Neither one of us spoke, and I could feel his heart pounding.

An owl broke the silence.

"I'm a good pilot, Dorothy," Red said. "I'll be okay."

"Oh, I know. I'm not worried about you," I said. "It's me I'm worried about." I was about to cry, and I didn't want to.

He needs me to be brave. He doesn't need having to wonder about how I can handle things while he's gone.

"I hate to leave you," he said.

"I know. I'll be okay." I snuggled closer to him, trying to draw from his strength.

I don't want him to worry about me. I want him to know things are under control at home, that I can handle it.

Because I can. I know I can. I have to. I wish we could stay on the mountain forever, but tomorrow we have to come down from the mountain and do what we have to do.

*   *   *

The memories from the mountain carried us through the next few weeks. The days flew by in a blur. Red was working longer hours as the squadron prepared to deploy. I was busy getting the boys ready to start school and finding a nursery school for Leslie. Before we knew it, it was October.

I was lying across the bed watching Red pack his bags. *We aren't supposed to be doing this. You were going to be a Navy pilot for four or five years, and then go home and be a baseball coach, remember?*

Aloud, I said, "Don't forget to pack your tape recorder."

Yes, I had learned how to cope well with my life as a Navy wife. But now Red was going to war, on the other side of the world. Mike was only eight years old. David, seven, had just entered first grade. We had celebrated Leslie's fourth birthday just before Red started packing. She wouldn't even remember him when he came home next June!

Would the mail come on schedule? I glanced over toward the dresser, at the new tape recorder Red had bought in the Navy Exchange to replace the one we'd worn out. His voice on tape would have to take his place for seven months. It would have to do.

He would be facing antiaircraft guns and missiles. *What are his chances of getting killed? Just how dangerous is flying missions over North Vietnam?* I tried to push these questions out of my mind and reached for one of Red's khaki shirts, folding it slowly.

As I came back to the present, I heard him giving me last-minute instructions.

"Don't forget to sign Mike up for Little League in the spring," he reminded me. "I'll be back in time to see the last two or three games. I think the Little League season goes into July, early July, anyway."

He was going off to war, and he was talking about baseball!

"Be careful, Red." I couldn't help saying it.

He leaned over the pile of uniforms on the bed and put his big, strong arms around me. I clung to him, fighting back the tears.

"Be brave for me, Dorothy," he said, holding me close.

Mercifully, I could not foresee how many years would pass before his arms would hold me again.

5

Presumed Captured

It was a long winter, and it was scary to think about Red flying combat missions. The air war over North Vietnam was intensifying and more and more U.S. fighter-bombers were going down behind enemy lines, many of them from Oceana-based squadrons. While the VA-35 squadron wives got together often and tried hard to bolster one another's morale, the talk invariably turned to the war and the lastest casualty. None of the squadrons had returned without losing at least one aircraft, and we knew that any day could bring news of the loss of one of our husbands. I tried not to think about the escalating air war. I knew Red was a good pilot and that he believed in his mission.

"It's my job," he'd said when I told him goodbye, "and we're over there to protect the South Vietnamese people from communist aggression. We have to draw a line somewhere, and we need to have a U.S. presence in that part of the world."

But from his tapes and letters I could tell that he was becoming more and more frustrated by the way the war was being conducted. He and the other pilots were risking their lives, flying through heavy antiaircraft fire and evading deadly radar-guided surface-to-air missiles, to bomb insignificant targets: storage facilities, truck repair depots, and the same bridges over and over again. They wanted to go after targets that would make a difference: the airfields, the SAM sites, the ships in Haiphong Harbor that they could see unloading military hardware with impunity. Their targets were chosen for political reasons by the White House and never, he said, by the military commanders in the field. Hanoi, where the enemy's command structure was located, was definitely off limits.

"In short," he said on one tape, "we're fighting this air war with our hands tied behind our backs. It's a tough way to fight a war. And it's probably going to last a long, long time."

I was learning that most of the flyers shared his frustration. They were "gung ho" naval aviators when they deployed, but when they returned, they were battle weary, disillusioned, and disheartened by the loss of fellow aviators over targets they considered worthless. Then most of them had to turn around and go back six months later and do it all over again: bomb the same targets—no victory in sight.

I also tried not to think about the war itself—and our reasons for fighting it. I knew it was Red's job, what he was trained to do, and what he was paid to do. I understood that a fighting man can't choose his own war. I wanted to believe this war was being fought for the right reasons, but it seemed to me that the reasons kept changing. Anti-war sentiment around the world and in the United States as well was becoming increasingly vocal, adding to my confusion. If the war was worth fighting, wasn't it worth winning? Were we asking young soldiers to give their lives for a losing cause? And what about pilots like Red who were sent to fly combat missions over targets that had no value?

I didn't have the leisure to dwell on these thoughts for long, though. I met the principal of Everett School, a private school in Virginia Beach, at a Christmas party. She was delighted to discover I was a teacher and offered me a job to complete the school year for a teacher who had resigned. Leslie could attend kindergarten free, and my hours would allow me to be home by the time the boys got home from school each day. I took the position, hoping it would keep me so busy that I wouldn't have time to worry about Red.

By January, the new job and the effort of trying to be both mom and dad to three youngsters made my life hectic. And I still found myself worrying about the combat missions. I could tell from his voice that Red was feeling the fatigue of flying missions every day, dodging missiles and flak. But by May, I had begun to relax a little. The weather was sunny and warm. School would soon be out. The children and I could spend long days at the beach and at the community pool. Best of all, this long deployment was almost over, and Red would be home in another six weeks or so!

I was really beginning to look forward to Fridays and the two-day break from school. When Leslie and I came home on Friday, May 19, we found three letters from Red waiting in the mailbox. I changed Leslie's clothes, put on my old pink-and-white checked bathing suit, and sat down in the sun on the patio to read the letters. Leslie headed for her new sandbox to build sand castles. Red's third letter said the line period was ending, and they were heading into the Philippines for some much-needed rest and recreation. *Good*, I thought, glancing at the date, *he's in the Philippines today. In a few days, they'll go back for one more line period and then they'll head home. It's almost over.*

The front doorbell rang. I left Leslie playing in the sandbox, walked through the house, and opened the front door. A naval officer in dress whites stood on the low front steps, his face pale.

"Red's down," he said.

I swayed, making an effort to concentrate on the man's face. Red was in the Philippines. I knew he was. The letter I was holding in my hand said he would be in the Philippines on May 19, Ho Chi Minh's birthday. "Sure do hate to miss Uncle Ho's birthday party, but I'm looking forward to the break," he'd said in his letter.

"Try to hang on," Commander Bill Small continued hastily, trying to lessen the shock. "Red had a good ejection. He made it to what they call a 'safe area.' I'm sure the Air Force search and rescue (SAR) people from Thailand will pick him up."

Only then did I notice the young Navy chaplain standing silent, a few short paces behind the commander. *Maybe they aren't so sure they'll pick him up*, I thought crazily, sinking into the small chair by the door. The chaplain's face was out of focus. Dimly, I heard him clear his throat.

"I wouldn't tell the kids just yet. Wait and see if they pick him up." His voice was shaking. *Poor men. This can't be easy for them, having to come to tell me this.* I tried to focus on Commander Small's face. He was asking me something.

"What time do the two boys get home from school? Isn't there a neighbor they could stay with until tomorrow morning?" I watched him sit down gingerly on the edge of the brown tweed sofa opposite me. "We'll probably be getting updates from the search and rescue people throughout the night. We'll be bringing them to you as they come in. It could get kinda hectic around here tonight."

I tried to concentrate. I had to understand what he was saying. His face was swimming in front of mine. I remembered Leslie. She must still be engrossed with her sand castle. *I should go check on her. I hope she doesn't come looking for me until these two harbingers of doom are gone. I need time to compose myself, to think, to decide what to tell her. How much can a four-year-old comprehend about the words "missing in action"?*

The house was rapidly filling up with squadron wives and neighbors wanting to help. I noticed Red's commanding officer's wife in the hallway. My good friend Laura Foote, whose husband was also in VA-35, was talking to the chaplain in the dining room. All the faces were a blur. Above the murmuring voices I suddenly heard the squealing brakes of the school bus that meant Mike and David would soon be running through the door, home from school. *Oh, God, what will I say to them?*

The boys bounded up the steps and into the front hall, slamming the glass storm door behind them. They looked around curiously at all the strange faces, and then, mercifully, headed for the refrigerator. *I'm glad I don't have to tell them now.* Before they could ask any questions, they were gone, whisked away by someone, I wasn't sure who, to stay overnight with neighbors. Leslie had come in behind them, trailing sand, and was hanging onto my knee, staring up at me.

Commander Small and the chaplain backed out of the room, promising to keep me posted. Laura offered to spend the night, and I accepted. I wasn't sure I should be alone in the house with a small child, not knowing what kind of message might come in the middle of the night.

After things had settled down and most of the people had

gone, Laura and I put Leslie to bed. Then we sat staring at the telephone willing it to ring. Surely the phone would ring any minute and someone would tell me the rescue people had found Red and picked him up. But the messages that came in throughout the long night to the communications people at NAS Oceana, which they immediately relayed to me, all said pretty much the same thing,

"Search and rescue operation still in progress."

I was impressed by the capability of NAS Oceana to be in constant communication with *Enterprise*, halfway around the world in the Gulf of Tonkin, and thankful that they were willing to share each message with me.

Finally, Laura told me to go to bed.

"Tomorrow's not going to be easy. The boys will be back and you'll have to talk to them," she said. "I'll listen for the phone and wake you the minute it rings."

Gratefully, I headed back to my room, leaving Laura by the phone. I lay down on my bed, trying to figure out what I would say to Mike and David in the morning. The chaplain had offered to come back in the morning to help me tell them.

"No, I'll tell them," I had said. I could see that he was relieved, and I didn't blame him. It would be a difficult thing to do.

Morning came too soon. I found Laura in the kitchen, pouring milk on Leslie's cereal.

"They just called again," she said. "Search and rescue is still in progress. I made coffee."

I poured myself a cup of the scalding liquid and sat down beside Leslie at the table. She gazed at me, her big blue eyes full of questions, as she put a spoonful of cereal into her mouth. *What am I going to tell her? And how long should I wait to do it?*

Mike came home around ten, and I followed him down the hall to his room.

This is going to be the hardest thing I've ever had to do, I thought.

Mike plumped down on his blue denim-covered bed and started untying one of his dirty white sneakers. His jaws moved furiously up and down, his mouth crammed full of pink bubble gum.

"Let me hold your gum, Mike." I was sitting on the other side of his bed.

"Why?" he asked, puzzled, handing me the sticky pink mass.

"Because you're probably going to cry." I took a deep breath. "I have some bad news about your dad."

Mike flinched, blue eyes wide.

"Is he dead?"

"No. I don't know. No. Well, I don't think so." I bit my lip, hard.

His nine-year-old fist pounded the pillow.

"Why does everything always happen to us?" he mumbled, his thin shoulders beginning to shake.

I stared at him. Then I realized with a start that he was talking about watching his beloved beagle puppy Penny run out into the street into the path of a speeding car, just a few days ago.

I put my arm firmly around his jerking shoulders and, as gently as I could, tried to explain that Red had parachuted into the jungle and had radioed to the planes overhead that he was safely on the ground.

"So we can think of him as alive, for now, anyway." I paused. "It's okay to cry, Mike," I added, hugging him with both arms.

Then I stood up and walked out of the room, quietly closing the door. His gasping sobs followed me into the hallway. I knew he'd want to be by himself to cry.

I found David in the back yard, playing with the cat from next door. *Good, he's alone. I need to tell him about Red now, before he hears me talking to someone else.*

"Dave," I began, "Sit here with me on the step. I want to talk to you about something."

"Is it bad?" David wanted to know. "Is that why you wouldn't look for a band-aid yesterday?"

"A band-aid? Why did you need a band-aid?"

"I hurt my knee. Look. See it? But you told me to go next door to get a band-aid."

I couldn't have done that, I thought. *I don't remember him asking me for a band-aid. Oh, God, I've got to get control of myself for the sake of these children!*

"I'm sorry, honey. How's your knee?" I murmured.

"It's okay now. Did something happen to Daddy?"

I pulled him down on the step beside me and tried to explain that Red's plane was down, but that he was alive and that we would just have to wait and see when he could come home. He started crying softly.

"Are you sure he's not dead?"

"I'm pretty sure, Dave. We'll ask God to keep him safe, okay?"

"Okay," he whispered, and snuggled up to me.

For four days we received periodic messages from Oceana that the search and rescue effort was still underway. On the fourth morning, Commander Small stood on the front steps again.

"Dorothy, the search and rescue effort is over. Red's status is 'presumed captured.'"

"What does 'presumed' mean?" I wanted to scream the words at him.

"He was alive when he hit the ground. So we have to assume he's a POW. It's better to list him as 'captured' rather than just 'missing.' But they'll keep the word 'presumed' in front of 'captured' on the casualty list until we get some kind of confirmation," he said sadly.

Already they were talking about my beloved as though he were a statistic on a casualty list. Categorizing him. Counting him. I wanted to tell them to keep looking for him, that he was out there somewhere, waiting. He *had* to be. But I knew it wouldn't do any good. The decision had already been made, on the other side of the world. He was already in the Pentagon computer that stored the casualty lists.

Mike didn't say anything when I told him the rescue effort was over. He just stared at me, stunned. But seven-year-old David had some questions.

"Does that mean he's dead?" he asked.

"No, that means the Vietnamese have probably captured him," I said. "We aren't sure."

"He could still be hiding somewhere out in the jungle," he suggested helpfully, blue eyes wide.

"Yes, David, he could be. But they don't think so. We just don't know, honey."

Late that same night, I heard him cry out in his sleep and went into his room.

"What's wrong, Davey?" I switched on the lamp beside his bed and rolled him over to face me. "Bad dream?"

He rubbed his eyes.

"I dreamed Daddy was fighting with a tiger," he wailed.

What can I say to him? He looked up at me, cheeks wet with tears, wide awake now.

"Mommy, what kind of hats do the Vietnamese soldiers wear?"

He couldn't pronounce Vietnamese. It came out "vet-ma-nese."

"I don't know, Dave." I hugged him close to me.

I told myself he didn't really want to know about the soldiers' hats, that he just wanted me to be there, to give him another good-night kiss. I lied to him, telling him I was sure everything would be all right, and lay down on the bed beside him until he went back to sleep.

The house was silent again. I tiptoed down the narrow hall, walked out the front door and sat down on the steps. Hands clasped around my knees, I looked through the tops of the tall pine trees into the murky black sky and realized suddenly that it was under that same endless sky, somewhere, that Red was struggling to survive whatever it was that was happening to him.

"He that dwelleth in the secret place of the Most High shall abide under the shadow of the Almighty," I had read in the Psalms.

"God," I whispered, "Red's in your secret place. Does your shadow reach all the way to Vietnam?"

The silent front steps would become my secret place, my wait-ing place. Night after night, after the children were in bed, I'd sit there, leaning against the rough bricks, hugging my knees. I would take solace from the stillness, and pray that some day, somehow, word would come to us that Red was still alive, and that the day would come when we'd see him again.

6

The "Keep-Silent" Rule

Attack Squadron 35 came home from Vietnam right on schedule, one sweltering day the first week in July.

Mike crouched at first base, eyes riveted on the batter, perspiration soaking his blue and yellow baseball uniform. The score was tied in the last game of the 1967 Little League season.

The worn wooden bench scratching my bare legs, I was wiping Leslie's flushed little face when I heard the A-6A Intruders roaring in the distance. *That's Red's squadron,* I thought. *They're going to fly right over the ball field.*

Then they were overhead, silver wings flashing in the hot sun. There should have been twelve planes, but there were only eleven. One was missing. One airplane and two men, Red and Kelly.

They'll have some news for me. Surely they will.

Six weeks had gone by since Commander Small had brought the message that Red was "presumed captured." Six weeks of screaming silence. Every morning for six weeks I had awakened thinking, *today I'll hear something.* But I hadn't. Surely someone from the squadron would have some idea about what might have happened to Red and Kelly.

I tried to concentrate on the game. Mike was staring up at the sky, baseball glove resting on his hip. *He knows that's Red's squadron,* I thought. *And his dad's not with them.*

One by one, in the days and weeks that followed, the aviators from VA-35 came to "pay their respects." It was uncomfortable for them. Groping for words, not wanting to look me in the eye, each in turn tentatively offered whatever encouragement he could.

Bob Miles was the most direct.

"I think he's still out there, Dorothy. The SAR teams fly over that area of the jungle every day. Red's tough. He's in excellent physical condition. I believe he'll make it. He might even be walking to Thailand. They'll find him." He tried to reassure me.

"What happened, Bob?" I wanted to know. "I thought the SAR teams were pretty good."

"They are, Dorothy," he said. "But they dropped the ball on this one."

All the guys think he's still in the jungle. They don't all say it, but that's what they think. Oh, God, he's still out there!

As the weeks went by, I saw less and less of the men from the squadron. It was awkward for them when I did see them. It was awkward for me, too. I didn't fit anymore. And they had their own problems. They'd been gone for seven months. They'd be going back into combat just after Christmas. I was a grim reminder to them—and to their wives—that some of them might not make it back next time. I didn't want to be a "hanger-on." I knew Navy widows who hung on to their husbands' squadrons, who just couldn't let go of the life they had known. I had always thought that was a mistake. I didn't want to do that, but it was lonely outside the squadron, and it was hard to decide where I did belong.

Weeks turned into months. *How can a man bail out of an airplane and just disappear from the face of the earth? Is he still hiding out there, trying desperately to get the attention of the SAR planes flying overhead? How long do those little survival radios work? Did some peasants find him and turn him over to the authorities? Is he still . . . alive?*

I refused to think of him as dead.

We were so close, I said to myself. *We were so close, I'm going to know it, some way I'm going to know it, if he's no longer alive. I need to follow the advice I gave David and think of him as alive, for now.* Or was that totally unrealistic? I ricocheted back and forth between hope and despair. *Should I encourage the children to hope, or help them face what seem to be the facts?*

And what are they doing in Washington? If Red's a POW, who is pressing the Hanoi government for information about him? Or is there

*any way to do that? How much should I expect for one man on the casu-
alty list?*

The official telegram I had received from the Navy, the one
confirming what Commander Small and the chaplain had told
me, also had cautioned me not to tell anyone except our immedi-
ate families that Red had been shot down over North Vietnam.
"For your husband's safety and well-being," the telegram said.
That was pretty persuasive language!

How my being so secretive about what had happened could
possibly benefit Red in any way, I couldn't imagine. Was it because
he might still be out there evading capture? Our whole world had
collapsed, but we weren't supposed to talk about it. That made it
really hard to explain to people what had happened, especially to
the people at my school and at the boys' school. The boys didn't
understand why they couldn't tell anyone about losing their dad.

"Is there something wrong with being shot down?" Mike asked
me. I had no idea how to answer him without adding to his fears.

I was puzzled by the official-sounding admonition to keep silent about Red's shoot-down, but I was sure the Navy knew more
than I did about the situation. I wasn't about to do anything, or
allow the children to do anything, that would jeopardize Red's
"safety and well-being."

Three months went by. Still there was no word. My sister
Mary Joe gave up her vacation and came to spend it with us. The
children and I loved her so much that she helped us all make it
through the summer. In early August, we went down to North
Carolina to spend two weeks with my parents.

My dad had taken Red's shoot-down especially hard. He was a
man of great faith and had stayed on his knees all night when we
got the news, beseeching God to let the rescue planes pick Red up.
When it didn't happen, he was devastated. He felt guilty, because
he thought he had somehow let me down when I needed him. I
needed to reassure him that the faith he had taught me when I was
a child was keeping me strong now. He couldn't go through this
ordeal for me, as much as he wanted to.

I realized I couldn't lean on my parents. I had to get back to
my own home, stand on my own two feet, and summon my own
strength and my own faith. When the two weeks were over, we

went back to Virginia Beach. I wrote a long letter to my dad, thanking him for teaching me about faith.

> ...since you feel that your faith failed me, I want to remind you that the faith I have was given to me *by you* in my early years. And at this moment of my own need, no one else's faith could possibly bring me through this. It could even be the will of God that you were not able to let me lean on you, because that would not have been sufficient. So you must thank Him that you were able to give me long ago what I need for this time in my life. I promise to call you if I need you, and I probably will need you desperately later. But now I must not lean on *anyone*. I love you and I am thankful for you.

I made plans to go to Washington before school began again in September. I wanted to talk to everyone who would see me, who might be able to tell me what to expect, or who might be able to tell me what the government was doing to find out about Red. The children would stay with friends in Washington while I made the daily rounds in the Pentagon and on Capitol Hill. I called before we left and made appointments with everybody I could think of who might be able to help. Navy officials, to start with. People in the State Department. Congressmen and senators.

I was intimidated by the important officials with the unfamiliar titles, hesitant about what to ask and how to ask it. I wanted so much to believe what each of them said, in one way or another:

"Trust us. We're doing everything we can."

None of them explained just what it was they were doing. Everyone was very solicitous, talking about how barbaric the North Vietnamese were not to even acknowledge the men being held as POWs. I got the distinct impression that I couldn't really expect to hear anything about Red until the war ended. But no one seemed to have any idea when that might be. It was a "limited engagement"; it could last indefinitely.

"But if they won't acknowledge holding him, they can't be held accountable for him when the war does end!" I protested to Commander Jenkins in the Bureau of Navy Personnel.

"That *is* a concern, Mrs. McDaniel," he said kindly. "Unfortunately, in most cases, the Hanoi government *doesn't* acknowledge holding men prisoner. So just the fact that they don't tell us Red's there doesn't mean he isn't."

I realized that Commander Jenkins was, in fact, doing everything *he* could. It was his job to try and explain the situation to worried wives and help with what the Navy called "casualty assistance": finances, legal advice, and other business and personal matters. I could see that his concern was genuine, and I knew I would need his help in the coming days. Navy casualty assistance was, I learned, outstanding, and I was grateful to those who worked so diligently to make my life easier as the wife of a missing serviceman.

But I needed to hear from the politicians and the bureaucrats responsible for policy what our government was doing to find out what had happened to Red and other missing men. The man I met with in the State Department told me he had "reason to believe" our POWs were being treated well, but he couldn't tell me what made him think so. He said he had no idea whether we would hear from Red or not. But the State Department was "doing everything we can" to determine Red's status. And the people I talked to on Capitol Hill seemed to know even less than I did about the war and how we planned to win it—or end it. Most of them were largely unaware of the fact that most of the American pilots who were shot down and classified as presumed captured were never heard from again.

"You mean you haven't heard from him?" one congressman asked me. "I was under the impression that POW families are allowed to receive mail. I saw a piece on TV made by an East German film crew that showed the POWs opening *their* mail. You might want to contact the International Red Cross."

I was astounded by his lack of knowledge.

"The Red Cross isn't allowed into Vietnam," I explained politely. There was nothing to be gained by being rude. I wanted to appear calm and in control so he wouldn't just dismiss me as an over-anxious wife.

"And the Hanoi government won't give the Red Cross the names of the prisoners," I continued. "It seems to me that our government needs to make some sort of big deal about their refusal to allow the Red Cross to inspect the camps, at least to find out who's in there."

"Well, I guess as long as we're bombing, we can't very well make any big deal about anything," he said. "But, Mrs. McDaniel, I want to assure you that I'll do everything I can."

Does someone write a script for these people? I wondered. *They all say the same thing. This one, too, will do "everything I can."* I wondered just what that would be, but I knew it was pointless to ask. In fact, the entire trip seemed pretty pointless. I didn't know what I had expected from all these meetings. Just to feel better, probably. To be reassured that, somewhere, someone wiser than I had things under control. But I was feeling worse by the minute, and I knew I couldn't afford to feel worse. I had to keep my spirits up, for the sake of the children. To be demoralized was to court disaster for my family and myself. I wanted to kick and scream. I wanted to cry. But I also wanted to be admitted to this man's office again when I thought of something specific he could do. So I thanked him profusely for seeing me and shook the hand he offered me, smiling broadly.

I decided to stay an extra day so I could take the children to the National Zoo. I had done everything I could think of to find out about Red. I would put him out of my mind for a day and concentrate on having some fun with the children. It had been a summer of turmoil for them. A day at the zoo would be good for all of us.

We were standing in front of a large cage watching two orange-and-black-striped tigers sun themselves on the gray rocks. A third tiger roamed around in the yellow sand, warily eyeing the jabbering tourists staring into the cage.

My eye fell on the little square map attached to the iron bars at the bottom of the tiger cage.

"Natural Habitat," the words above the map of Southeast Asia screamed at me.

He's still out there! My heart was in my throat. *The guys in the squadron think Red's still out there in the jungle. I should go to the Pentagon and tell someone there to make sure they're still looking for him. But who would I tell? Who would listen to me and not just write me off as one more distraught POW wife?*

As Mike, David, and Leslie, absorbed with their zoo adventure, pulled me from cage to cage to see the man-eating tigers, the poisonous reptiles, the unfamiliar wild animals from all over the world, I found myself studying the little maps, making mental lists of the dangers lurking in the jungle areas where Red might still be hiding even now, after all this time.

Dave won't be the only one dreaming about tigers, I thought. *Oh, God, where is he? Oh, dear God, I <u>am</u> acting like a distraught wife!*

"Let's go, gang," I said abruptly. "It's getting late. Let's go get a hot dog. I want to get out of town before rush hour starts."

Mike looked up at me.

"What's the matter, Mom?" he asked. He stared down at the little map on the python cage, and then fell silent, his lips becoming a grim line in his freckled face. Protectively, he took Leslie by the hand as the four of us headed up the rocky path.

He knows what I'm thinking, I said to myself, as we got into line at the hot dog stand. *Poor Mike. At nine, he's supposed to be secure and carefree, but he thinks it's up to him to hold this family together.*

I remembered that the week after Red was shot down, Mike had asked my sister Mary Joe to take him to the flower shop. He used the money he was saving for a new baseball glove to buy me a bunch of white daisies.

"I need to help Mom be happy," he had explained matter-of-factly to Mary Joe.

"Take care of Mommy for me, Mike," Red had said to him in front of the campfire in the mountains. He had said it again that October morning when we were driving him to Oceana to meet the squadron for deployment to Vietnam. *I wish he hadn't said that. I'm the parent. Mike's not supposed to take care of me; I'm supposed to take care of him.*

All summer, Mike had been studying my face with his too-knowing eyes. I was sure that he knew even now that my mind had wandered away, that I was thinking about his dad out there in the jungle on the other side of the world.

*   *   *

That first tentative trip to Washington was the first of many I would make. Sometimes one or two of the other POW/MIA wives from Virginia Beach would join me. In between trips, we tried to learn as much as we could about the war, about the structure of the Washington bureaucracy, about who really wielded the power in each office, which undersecretary did what, and who in Congress really cared. Sometimes we'd rehearse our uncertain lines before we got there.

"You be you, and I'll be the man in the State Department," I said to Janie Tschudy as soon as we'd buckled our seat belts early one morning in February 1968. We took turns playing the role of the official who manned the POW/MIA desk in the State Department. First Janie would rehearse her questions, and I would try to anticipate what he would say. Then Janie would play the man in the State Department and I would practice my questions.

We had to get up early, to pick up our babysitters and reach the airport in time to catch the seven o'clock flight to Washington. All the rushing around and the tense rehearsal on the plane made both of us a little giddy by the time we were ushered into the huge mahogany-paneled office and seated in front of the large polished desk. Nervously fingering my white faux pearls, I went first.

"Sir," I began. "What is our government doing to pressure the Hanoi government for the names of the American pilots they're holding? Just his *name*. I'll settle for that, for now."

The man who'd been assigned the very unpleasant task of meeting with the POW wives who visited the State Department began to intone, once again, the complicated provisions of the Geneva Accords, and why the North Vietnamese didn't believe they should have to adhere to the convention protecting prisoners of war. No war had been declared, and the Hanoi government considered the downed pilots not POWs, but "war criminals."

From the corner of my eye, I saw Janie's hand slip up to her mouth. I knew she was hiding a grin. In his best diplomatic manner, the man behind the desk was saying almost verbatim what she'd said he would say. I didn't dare look at Janie. I knew we'd both burst out laughing.

The diplomatic voice droned on. We had to be patient, he said. The State Department was engaged in critical high-level negotiations with almost every government in the world, seeking information and better treatment for the men Hanoi was holding.

He wished so much he could tell us about it, but it was all so very complicated and, of course, highly classified.

Now we were beginning to giggle. Janie stood up, looking pointedly at her watch.

"We have to run, Dorothy. We'll miss our flight."

The poor harried man peered at us curiously over his massive desk as we made our hasty exit, wondering, I was certain, just what he could have possibly said that we thought was so funny.

As soon as we turned the corner of the long white marble corridor, both Janie and I leaned against the wall, doubled over with laughter, tears of hysteria and pent-up anxiety pouring down our cheeks.

I envied Janie. She'd had several letters from Bill, who was shot down early in the air war over North Vietnam. I thought getting a letter from Red, if he *was* alive and being held in a POW camp, would be the most wonderful thing that could possibly happen to me. I knew if he hadn't been taken prisoner, he couldn't still be alive. It had been almost a year. No man could survive that long in a hostile jungle. Surely he was in one of the POW camps. He had to be. I knew I had to get the Hanoi government to admit they were holding him in order to delete the "presumed" in front of the "captured" on the computer printouts listing him as a U.S. casualty. Then Red's captors would have to keep him alive, knowing they would be held accountable for him when the war was over.

Janie and I decided not to waste time eating lunch. We wanted to have enough time to make the rounds on Capitol Hill. We were never sure meeting with the congressmen did any good, but we didn't want to let them forget the POWs and the men who were still missing. By the time we were settled in our seats on the five o'clock flight back to Norfolk, we were exhausted—and ravenous. The flight attendant was startled when we each helped ourselves to an entire handful of tiny tea sandwiches from the tray she extended to us just as the plane reached cruising altitude.

"Janie," I said, popping a sandwich into my mouth. "I think we're going to have to do it ourselves."

"I know," Janie mumbled, her mouth stuffed with watercress and cream cheese. "Nobody's talking about them. I wish I knew what Bill would want me to do."

"I'm not sure how much we *can* do, Janie," I said, settling back into the brown cushioned seat.

But I was sure of one thing now. The keep-silent rule had been designed primarily to keep the pressure off the politicians, and it wasn't going to do a thing for Red and me.

7

The World
Is Watching!

I was devastated to realize that the people in the State Department and on Capitol Hill, and maybe even in the White House, were not working around the clock to do something about the POWs. In my naiveté I had believed the bureaucrats when they said, "We're doing all we can." I didn't press them when they said they just couldn't tell us about all the secret negotiations and other "high level" activities. I didn't even know what they *could* do. I understood that Red couldn't come home until the war ended, but I felt sure that something could be done to find out if he was in one of the POW camps—and if he was, to force the Hanoi government to say so.

I was about to learn an important lesson about public opinion. Public opinion isn't restricted to democratic nations. Even the communist regime in Hanoi could be moved by world opinion. A small group of American service wives and mothers could start a movement that would pry open heavy prison doors on the other side of the world—and in the process of putting pressure on Hanoi, could make their sons and husbands so important to the American people that the politicians would have to bring them home when the war was over.

I was also about to learn an important lesson about government, about democracy. Simply stated, the lesson was this: the biggest fire is the one that gets attention. In a democratic government, what the people are talking about is what gets action from the politicians. It seemed impossible that the men and women who governed would not, as a matter of course, do whatever needed to be done. But I realized this was the ideal. In reality, one of democracy's greatest strengths is that in a government "by the people," the people are the ones who make things happen.

None of this was clear on that blustery February day in 1968. Back then, I only knew that no one cared as much as we did. I was certain I would never see Red again if I couldn't figure out a way to get his name on the books as a confirmed prisoner of war.

One man in Washington did seem to care almost as much as we did. Commander Bob Boroughs worked in the Pentagon, behind heavy unmarked doors. Scuttlebutt from other POW wives said he was in Naval Intelligence. The first time I met with him, he asked, "Who told you about me?"

"All the wives know about you," I responded hesitantly, suddenly aware that this meeting would be a cat-and-mouse game, that he would be testing me.

"And what do they know about me?" he asked, eyeing me warily.

"That you offer guidance about making inquiries through various channels like the anti-war groups and newspaper reporters who travel to Hanoi," I ventured, timidly.

"Who told you that?"

"I would say it's common knowledge among the POW wives," I said. "We have a pretty good grapevine."

"That's for sure." His eyes twinkled. "Well, I can't advise you on any of that stuff. But try me any time, I'm a good listener.

"You're right about one thing," he continued. "You've got to get Hanoi to say they're holding him. And you're the one who can do that. The government can't do that for you."

"Listen, I'd talk to the devil himself to find out about Red. I'll do anything I have to do—as long as it won't harm Red or make things worse for him," I said.

He grinned, but said nothing. Now I had the direction I needed, unofficial as it might have been. I had found an ally in the Pentagon, someone who seemed to want to find out about Red as much as I did. And I had a strong suspicion that I had found a maverick bureaucrat, one who didn't buy the keep-silent rule.

It was easy to find out who in the anti-war movement would be traveling to Hanoi, and which reporters were going in. All I had to do was comb through the newspapers and news magazines. It was harder to find addresses of the individuals who weren't with the news media, but I could usually get their telephone numbers through information. The anti-war activists I talked to were skeptical. They believed that if the Hanoi government hadn't allowed Red to write to us, then he probably wasn't in one of the camps. They assured me that the North Vietnamese had a policy of "humane and lenient" treatment toward the "aggressor pilots who are bombing their country."

"Oh, no," I responded. "I can't reveal how I know where Red is. But we have positive information that he is being held incommunicado by the North Vietnamese, that he is in solitary confinement." I took a deep breath. Lying didn't come easy to me, and it was so important that I sound convincing.

"I'm not asking you to find out where he is. I know where he is. I'm asking you to find out about his health. I want you to ask the North Vietnamese why they won't allow him to contact us. I want to know if he is being mistreated, that kind of thing. If you don't want to ask about him, would you take a letter to him from me and just hand it to somebody in the government?"

"Why don't you just mail it to Hanoi? Vietnam's a civilized country. The international mail does go to Hanoi, you know," the voice on the phone would say patronizingly.

"Oh, I do mail letters to him. But I don't think he gets them."

With that, I could usually get the voice on the phone to agree to take a letter to Red into Hanoi. Then I planned the letter very carefully:

Dear Eugene, [Very formal, no secret messages here.] We are so thankful to know you are alive. [Not true, but necessary.] How is your health? [Hanoi, we know you have him!] We are well and happy. [Innocuous, fills up a line.] The children are growing. [He has a family; let him write to us!] We hope to hear from you soon. [Again, we know you have him!] Keep faith and never forget how much we love you. [In the unlikely event that he actually gets this.]

Dorothy

I wrote the letters, not to Red, but to his captors. *If I say it often enough,* I thought, *they'll believe I know more than I actually do, and they'll keep him alive. They might, by some miracle, even decide to let him write to us.*

I was sure I had unofficial permission from my end to send such letters, but I was afraid I might be putting unwanted pressure on Red to write to us. Resisting would be of the utmost importance to him. His captors were probably telling him he would be allowed to write to us if he would sign a confession of his "war crimes," or make a statement condemning U.S. involvement in Vietnam, which would then be used for propaganda purposes.

But I have to take that chance, I reasoned. *I wish I knew what Red would want me to do, but he can't tell me. This is a decision I have to make. I'm absolutely convinced that his only protection is an admission by the Hanoi government that they are holding him. So I have to take the chance that my meddling might put added pressure on him. I do have to take that chance...don't I?*

The decision to go public with my personal story—to expose my family to public scrutiny—was even scarier. The official instructions to stay home and be quiet "to protect your husband's safety" had lost their authority for me after the first year of waiting for word from Red. *That directive doesn't make any sense,* I thought. *The Vietnamese know he was shot down. If they didn't know it already, I've told them in all those letters. So how am I protecting Red's safety by keeping quiet? But good people who care about us, who know a lot more about it than I do, are telling me to stay out of the limelight.* I couldn't just ignore a conversation I'd had with one of Red's former commanding officers, a man Red and I both greatly respected.

"Dorothy," he'd said. "I know Red like I know my own son, and I *know* he would want you to be quiet, to stay home and take care of the kids. That's your role and that's what Red expects you to do. For God's sake, do what the Navy says! You'll just cause more problems for Red if you don't."

This advice from people I trusted and respected was hard to ignore. I was going against the experts, but I had to follow my instincts and my heart.

I was convinced that the North Vietnamese government would respond to public opinion. My belief was supported by the fact that every few months, one of the sympathetic-to-their-cause reporters would be invited to Hanoi to do a story about the "humane and lenient" treatment of the American "war criminals." Obviously, the opinion of the American people mattered to them. These propaganda pieces, orchestrated by the Hanoi government, received wide distribution in the United States. I remembered the congressman telling me he had seen POWs on TV opening their mail.

I picked the boys up from school the minute the Friday afternoon dismissal bell rang signaling the beginning of the Christmas holidays. We headed for my parents' home in North Carolina, the car loaded with presents and secret Santa toys. I couldn't get out of town fast enough. Holidays were still tough for me, and I needed my family around for moral support.

That Saturday morning, I walked down to the little post office in my hometown to pick up the mail. One of my parents' neighbors was driving down the street. She stopped when she saw me and rolled down her car window.

"Dorothy, I saw on TV that the POWs in Hanoi are getting good treatment. Did you see it? They were opening their letters from home. Some of them were playing ping-pong. It was Thanksgiving, and they were having a turkey dinner. They all looked healthy and happy," she said into the winter morning. "I was hoping you saw it. It made me feel so much better about Red."

I tried to explain to her that the film wasn't true, that I didn't believe Red was getting that kind of treatment, that the film she had seen was for public consumption, for *her* consumption and for the congressman's consumption.

"I haven't heard a thing from Red, Jeanne. They won't even acknowledge his presence there," I told her.

I could see she wasn't convinced. No doubt she was thinking that, if we hadn't heard anything, Red was probably not in one of the camps. But she was too kind to say so.

The propaganda piece seemed to be just one more example of Hanoi's sensitivity on the POW issue. If the North Vietnamese weren't sensitive to public opinion, why would they go to such lengths to show the POWs to the world? I felt certain that we could use this sensitivity to our men's advantage. If the wives and families of the missing men were to call Hanoi's bluff, perhaps the result would be some information about our husbands and sons, maybe even better treatment for them.

But calling Hanoi's bluff meant publicly parading ourselves and our sorrow. We would have to be emotional to get the press to write human interest stories about us. We might even have to cry on camera, on demand. I could think of nothing worse. I wasn't even sure I could do it.

They'll probably show Red everything I do and tell him everything I say, I feared. *It could be his undoing.* Was this the reason for the keep-silent rule? Was this what they meant by "for your husband's welfare and safety"?

I was sure the Navy hadn't made the keep-silent rule; the Navy was just carrying out the policy of the White House and the State Department. The assurances from the White House and the State Department about "negotiations" and "trust" and "we're doing everything we can" were beginning to ring hollow. Most of the congressmen we had met with the first year seemed just as uninformed now as they had when we first started making the rounds on Capitol Hill. Sometimes we felt as though we were educating them, not just on the POW/MIA issue, but on the war itself.

I knew I was in over my head trying to decide what to do. In my thirty-three years, most of my decisions had been made for me—or Red and I had made them together. Now I was on my own.

And what about the children? All four of us would be in the public eye. What would their mother's public exposure do to Mike, David, and Leslie? And what about *their* public exposure? I would have to use them in the stories, to get the human interest angle the press demanded. How would this affect them?

But how could I sit back and not try? I believed that Red's life was on the line.

*   *   *

Louise Mulligan called me the morning after I got back from my next trip to Washington.

"I'm getting the POW/MIA wives together Friday night at my house," she said. "We'll make it potluck, and you can report on your trip."

"I'll be there," I said. "But there's not much to report, just more of the same. Sometimes I think these Washington trips are a waste of time and money, Louise."

"No way," she replied. "The alternative is to just let the politicians forget about us and our men. Anyway, I have some new ideas from Sybil that I want to pass along. The wives from Hampton will be here, too."

The wives from Hampton were POW/MIA wives whose missing husbands had been stationed at Langley Air Force Base across the bay from Virginia Beach. Sybil was Sybil Stockdale, a POW wife who lived in San Diego. She had asked Louise to be coordinator in our area for an unofficial league of POW/MIA families she was trying to organize. Periodically, Sybil sent letter-writing suggestions to coordinators like Louise scattered around the country, who would pass them along to other POW/MIA families. The league was loosely structured, but it was growing rapidly. POW/MIA families told other families about this network which shared information and provided moral support for each other. And it was slowly becoming an activist group. None of us were brave enough—yet—to defy the keep-silent rule. We stuck to writing letters and asking our friends to write letters. We asked the newspaper editors, foreign ambassadors, and U.S. officials on Sybil's list to talk about our sons and husbands, but we were afraid to talk about them ourselves.

We were edging closer to telling our stories publicly, however. At Louise's house on Friday, several of us agreed that sooner or later, to make our letter-writing campaigns effective, we would have to make speeches and agree to media interviews. We decided there would be safety in numbers; if several of us went public at the same time, no one's husband would be singled out for special harassment. All of us were painfully aware that anything we said publicly in the United States would very likely be repeated to our husbands in Hanoi.

I made my first speech in November of 1968. Red had been missing for seventeen months, and we were no closer to finding out if he was dead or alive. I had bombarded Hanoi with one inquiry after another.

Richard Nixon had just been elected president of the United States. Since Red's plane had gone down, U.S. policy in Southeast Asia had fluctuated between on-again, off-again bombing of North Vietnam and nonproductive "peace initiatives." Then it was back to escalated bombing and increased fighting in South Vietnam. The stalemate had defeated President Johnson, had kept him from seeking reelection. The anti-war movement was growing. America had decided not to win the war and both presidential candidates had promised to end U.S. involvement in Southeast Asia. President-elect Nixon had talked a lot in his campaign about his "secret plan to end the war."

Well, Mr. President, your secret plan will have to include bringing home the POWs, I said to myself. *We're going to get them on the front pages of America's newspapers. We're going to talk about Hanoi's inhumanity, but we're also going to make sure U.S. policymakers are constantly reminded of our sons and husbands, and how long they've been in their prison cells and bamboo cages.*

I sounded pretty brave. But that November night before my first speech, I had a bad case of the jitters. *Speaking to a small group of church women can't hurt,* I told myself.

Well, it probably wouldn't help much, either. Was it worth the effort? And where would it lead?

The children were asleep, and I stood at the kitchen sink finishing up the dinner dishes. At eye-level was the little black wrought-iron plaque I had hung above the sink when Red left for Vietnam. The words of the "Serenity Prayer" etched on the metal seemed especially pertinent tonight.

"God, grant me serenity to accept the things I cannot change, courage to change the things I can, and wisdom to know the difference."

I looked past the prayer and out the window, through the branches of the pine trees and out into the night sky.

"Please, God, if speaking out is not the way to go, please, God, I need to find that out now."

The small group of church women turned out not to be so small. Every seat in the fellowship hall was taken, and a few women were standing. The women listened soberly to my appeal to help the POW/MIA families focus public attention on our men, the men we called "the forgotten men of the Vietnam War." Gripping the podium with both hands, I tried to read the expressions on their faces. I was sure they had never heard a plea like mine before, and I wondered what they thought of me. I ended my speech with a line from one of the prayers of Peter Marshall, a former chaplain for the U.S. Senate.

"Let us not be content to wait and see what will happen, but give us the determination to make the right things happen."*

For a moment there was silence. Then the women burst into applause, and they all started talking at once. Almost to a woman, this group wanted to know what they could do to help. They offered their time and their money. Some of them had some very creative ideas for ways to get publicity. They seemed to understand exactly what we needed to do.

I accepted the women's enthusiasm as confirmation from God that I had made the right decision. With no holds barred, I jumped into the public arena that Sybil and Louise and some of the other wives and mothers had already entered. We talked to everyone who would listen—and to some who wouldn't.

Not everyone was as receptive as the women in the church group. Some Americans agreed with Hanoi that the downed pilots were indeed war criminals, participating in an illegal war, and that they deserved the punishment they were receiving. Many who were sympathetic to the plight of the POWs just did not believe talking about them would do any good. They saw the North Vietnamese as barbarians who didn't care about American public opinion. But once I jumped into the limelight, I was willing to go anywhere and speak to any group that would allow me to come.

When we first started making speeches and appearing on television, two or three of the POW/MIA wives usually would go together. One would speak and the others would answer questions, pass out brochures, and provide moral support. After we grew accustomed to the public appearances and were speaking more often, we had to go alone.

---

*McGraw-Hill. The Prayers of Peter Marshall, p. 208.

Late one afternoon I picked up Jane Denton and drove to a small country town about an hour away from Virginia Beach to speak to a group of businessmen. I told my story, emphasizing that we knew Red was in one of the camps. If the North Vietnamese were going to hear what I said in this obscure Virginia town, I wanted them to think I knew more than I actually did, that I had some kind of intelligence information about Red's whereabouts.

"The North Vietnamese keep telling the world about their 'humane and lenient' treatment of the prisoners they're holding. If that is true," I asked the men, who were leaning forward and listening intently, "why won't they let me hear from him?"

Most of the men nodded their heads in agreement. I could see they were really with me.

"You can help us pry open those heavy prison doors so the world can see what is going on behind them," I continued, my voice growing stronger. "We are asking you to write letters to the North Vietnamese in Hanoi and in Paris. Write letters to foreign embassies and to the editors of newspapers. And don't forget to write to your congressmen and senators and ask them what they are doing to get information about our POWs.

"The brochures Mrs. Denton is passing out have addresses and sample letters. Please, help us make sure our men are not forgotten. *Don't let them be forgotten!*"

The applause was deafening. The men jumped to their feet.

Good, I thought, *a standing ovation. I must have gotten through to them. Not bad, Dorothy.*

I stood there smiling at them until the applause died down.

"Now, do you have any questions?" I asked bravely, very pleased with myself.

A tall man in a well-tailored suit seated at one of the front tables stood up. During my speech, I had noticed that he seemed to hang on my every word.

"Mrs. McDaniel," he said kindly, his eyes glistening with tears, "I appreciate your coming to speak to us, and you have my deepest sympathy. But what can we do about it?"

Patiently, I repeated everything I had just asked them to do. The skeptical look on his face told me that he just did not believe writing letters would do any good at all. *If I asked him to get a gun, go to Hanoi, break into the prison, and rescue the POWs by force, he would probably go,* I thought. *But he's not going to write any letters.*

Jane and I were hoping we'd get an honorarium, or at least a small check to pay for our gas. We were using our savings to pay for printing brochures and bumper stickers, as well as for travel. We didn't ask for money, but sometimes the groups we spoke to did give us a few dollars. This group, however, rewarded us with a huge home-baked coconut cake, a sugar-cured country ham, and a wood and brass plaque containing their national emblem.

As we drove back to the Beach, I said to Jane, "We didn't get through to them, you know. But at least we won't starve to death. Do you want the ham or the cake?"

Jane laughed.

"Do you think we could send the food to Red and Jerry?"

At least we can still laugh, I thought. *We laugh to keep from crying. But even that is something.*

Jane and I had become good friends as we had agonized over the decision about our public involvement in the POW/MIA effort. She was hesitant, as I was, to get into the public eye for fear of putting added pressure on the men. Her instincts were usually pretty good, and I looked to her for guidance. She occasionally prevented me from doing something impulsive, without thinking it through. Jane and Jerry had seven children, ranging from toddler to college age. She was rearing her large family alone, and doing it well. We spent many soul-searching hours together, determined to find the right course of action, then planning the POW/MIA campaigns, sharing the frustration of caution and indecision, sometimes ending up in tears. Tonight it was good to laugh with her.

That experience convinced me that my speech needed some work. The next time I spoke, I was much more dramatic. Members of the Virginia Beach Junior Chamber of Commerce wanted to get the national JayCees to start a POW/MIA publicity campaign. They asked me to speak to the local chapter to help convince the other members that the national campaign was a good idea. I got right to the point.

Gentlemen, my husband has a been a prisoner of war in North Vietnam for two and one-half years. I have never heard from him. I have made many inquiries about his health—through the International Red Cross, through travellers to Hanoi, and directly to North Vietnamese diplomats. None of my inquiries have been answered.

There is a door in Hanoi that I want to open. The door has a false front; the people who hold the key would have the world believe that everything is fine behind it. But there is mounting evidence that untold horror exists behind that door. It is the door to a prison camp where an unknown number of Americans wait—and wait—and wait.

Then I talked about my belief that world opinion could have an impact on the North Vietnamese government, and why I thought so. I gave statistics about the missing men, stressing the discrepancy between the numbers presumed to be in the camps and the numbers Hanoi had acknowledged.

A tiny hairline crack may have been made in that door in Hanoi when some POW/MIA wives went to Paris recently, asking "Are we wives or widows?" They were received cordially by North Vietnamese diplomats because the world was watching. Now North Vietnam has said a list of prisoners is forthcoming and all the families need do is write for information about the status and health of their loved ones. These promises were made because the world was watching. Perhaps my inquiry about my husband's state of health will be answered—if the world continues to watch. I want the world to be watching when those answers do or do not come. I want the world to be watching when and if that list arrives and is or is not authentic. I want the world to be watching for proof of Hanoi's claims of humanitarian treatment of prisoners of war.

The JayCees' effort to keep the POW/MIA issue before the public will ensure that the world continues to watch, and will help us open that prison door.

The JayCees adopted "The World is Watching!" as the theme of their POW/MIA campaign. The logo on their letterheads and bumper strips was an eye with a globe-shaped world as the iris.

The fact that the JayCees chose their motto from my speech really turned me on. It was easy to get discouraged when we recognized the magnitude of the task we had assigned ourselves: to focus world attention on our sons and husbands, create a national campaign to make certain they were not forgotten, and bring enough grassroots power to bear on the politicians that any solution to the war had to include the release of the POWs. But we kept at it. We knew we had to. Even though it looked like an impossible task, we knew we had to do it.

Our message spread. The speech I made to the group of church women led to an invitation to speak to the King's Daughters' national convention in Memphis. The King's Daughters, a national women's service organization, paid my expenses, which helped a lot. The mayor of Memphis met my flight and presented me with a key to the city. There was a lot of press coverage in Memphis, and the King's Daughters published our appeal in their national newsletter, which reached thousands of activist women across the nation.

Interviews on local Norfolk television stations led to an invitation to appear on "The Phil Donahue Show," then still a regional show in the Ohio-Michigan-Indiana area. The Donahue Show sent me and the two other wives who appeared on the show first-class airline tickets to Dayton, provided hotel accommodations, and even paid for our baby-sitters! Our first big mailing list was compiled from the responses we received from our Donahue appearance.

The men who had given us the cake and the ham sent us a small check; some of them became our most faithful letter writers. They decided to give us the benefit of the doubt and write the letters, even if they didn't believe their efforts would help.

It was harder to convince newspaper editors to do what we felt was needed. They wanted to interview us, take pictures of our children, and tell about our agony. But they couldn't see the value of the editorials and feature stories we wanted them to write, pieces which would condemn Hanoi's attitude toward the POWs and tell readers how to help. We made many personal visits to editors all over the country to present our case. They'd listen courteously and then ask, "Well, what do you want me to do?"

"Write about them in your newspaper," we'd respond. But we could see most of them thought we were grasping at straws.

They're the opinion-makers, I said to myself. *Surely they can see the power of public opinion.* But I had to admit, even to myself, that writing letters didn't sound like a very strong approach to what seemed the insurmountable obstacle of the Hanoi government's stubborn silence.

It was grassroots America that understood. As public interest in us grew, the press interest followed. At first the press coverage was sporadic; human interest stories in the small town newspapers of communities where POW/MIA families lived and an occasional local radio or TV interview with a POW/MIA wife or mother. Then the national networks and the big papers began to do stories. It seemed that press coverage was contagious, or at least highly competitive. We could usually get a paper to do a story by showing the editor the work another paper had done. I had always thought of the press as a corps of independent thinkers who led the way in forming public opinion. Now it appeared to me that most people in the media followed other people in the media. Once we recognized this, we were able to get our stories in more and more papers and the big magazines. Our postage bills mounted as the POW/MIA family network shared huge stacks of news clips with one another. We used these clips to entice other editors to write stories about us and about our missing men.

The POW/MIA wives and families worked day and night at spreading our message. We tried to measure our progress not by the size of the task ahead, but by how far we had come from the beginning. We continued to talk about our sons and husbands and fathers, and our message was always the same:

"Don't let them be forgotten!"

I always added my own personal note, my message to Hanoi.

"I know the North Vietnamese are holding my husband. Why won't they let him write to me?"

8

The Front Page

The letter from Red came on the same day the moon came between the earth and the sun. The solar eclipse captured the attention of most of the people in the Tidewater (Virginia) area, and the front page of the Norfolk *Virginian Pilot* was devoted almost entirely to coverage of this once-in-a-lifetime phenomenon.

But down at the very bottom of the front page, a tiny photograph of Commander Eugene "Red" McDaniel, taken just before he left for Vietnam, appeared alongside a small headline:

"A Wife's Belief Is Given Life."

The article was about how long Red had been missing and how his family had always believed he was alive. We were front page news! Even on the day Tidewater experienced a solar eclipse, we had made the front page. The caption under the picture of Mike, David, Leslie and me on the inside page stated, "The Mc-Daniel family has new hope."

Later on, the newspaper offered reduced-in-size copies of the front page filled with the story of the eclipse to local school libraries and classrooms. Red McDaniel's tiny picture would be framed and hung in seventh-grade classrooms all over Tidewater. I decided this was only fitting for what was surely a much more significant event than a solar eclipse.

The father of one of Mike's classmates was our mailman. Brad Yeager's dad had spotted the letter from Red as he was sorting out the next day's mail delivery and he had made a special trip to bring it to me that night. Standing on the front steps in the twilight, he held out the crumpled, flimsy envelope to me with trembling hands.

"I thought you'd want to have this tonight," he said.

I looked at the dirty-white envelope with the strange-looking postmark, "Hanoi, Vietnam." The return address read, "Camp of Detention for U.S. Pilots Captured in the Democratic Republic of Vietnam."

Shaking violently, I slowly unfolded the fragile scrap of paper, almost afraid to look.

Six short lines, words crowded together, scrawled with a scratchy ballpoint pen in a once-familiar left-handed slant, leapt off the page at me.

Dear Dorothy, Michael, David, Leslie, My health
is good in all respects—no permanent injuries.
You are my inspiration. Children, work, study, play
hard, help each other and Mommy be strong for our
reunion. Invest savings in mutual funds and stock.
Your decisions are mine. Dorothy, I love you deeply, Eugene.

15 December 1969

He was alive!

He was locked up in a dirty, lonely cell in a POW camp. Everything I had learned told me he was probably in solitary confinement, going through the kind of terrible torture I didn't dare think about. Why did he say he had no "permanent" injuries? What kind of injuries did he have? Why did he tell me what to do with our savings? Was he afraid he wasn't going to make it, that the children and I would need the money? Or perhaps it was a good sign, perhaps he was making plans for what we'd do with our savings when he came home.

No, I wouldn't analyze it, or try to read between the lines. I would just hold it close and be thankful for it. After three years of trying to find out if he was dead or alive, we knew he was alive!

Because we had made his name a household word, the letter from Red McDaniel postmarked Hanoi was front page news. And that meant Mike, David, Leslie, and I were front page news as well.

I was certain Red's letter was a direct result of my public activity. If the Hanoi government was really aware of my activities, as I had been told by the government people who are supposed to know about such things, then Red's captors thought I already knew he was in one of the camps. The North Vietnamese finally had acknowledged my questions. I believe they really did think I knew more than I did. For some reason known only to them, they had decided to let one of Red's letters come through.

All the hard work, the grueling, emotionally-draining speech-making and public appearances had finally resulted in the six-line letter from Red. He was alive! He was alive, and the North Vietnamese had admitted he was alive. To me, that meant they couldn't let him die.

However, it also meant more public exposure, more speeches, more television appearances, and more being away from Mike, David, and Leslie. I longed to protect the children from the images they must have carried in their minds about Red, where he was, what was happening to him. I had no answers to their questions. I was afraid to reassure them, to promise them everything would be all right. I wasn't sure that everything would be all right, and I knew it was better for them to accept the truth.

Mike, at twelve, was still trying not to cry. He had started his own "Don't Let Them Be Forgotten!" campaign at school. Now a seventh-grader, he was president of the student body of his elementary school. He had saturated the school with "Don't Let Them Be Forgotten!" brochures, bumper stickers, and pins, and many of the youngsters were writing letters and signing petitions and mailing them to Hanoi and Paris. Mike worked at the campaign as though it were all up to him to get his dad home. I worried. *That can't be good for a twelve-year-old. And the last thing he needs is to hear his mom on television talking about the brutality of the Vietnamese communists who are holding his dad.*

David, an imaginative first-grader when Red's plane was shot down, had fought battles for his dad on the brown-flecked white linoleum squares that made up the floor of our family room. Scores of little green plastic soldiers would stand in formation along the wall directly opposite the red brick fireplace. In front of the hearth, one plastic warrior would stand alone, ready to fight. Every time, the one lone soldier would beat the odds and win the battle.

Now that he was ten, Dave fought his battles on the playground at school. I had warned him the last time he had gotten into a schoolyard fight that the consequences would be severe if it happened again.

"David," I said when he came in from school. "Your teacher called. She tells me you've been fighting again. Tell me about it."

"Billy said my dad's dead," he muttered.

"Why would Billy say that?" I asked. "Tell me everything that happened."

"I told him that Daddy used to be a heavyweight boxing champion and that he played professional baseball before he went to Vietnam," he hung his head and stared at the tips of his sneakers.

"David, that isn't true. Why would you tell him something like that?"

"Well, Billy's always bragging about his dad. And *you* told me Daddy played pro ball," he said defiantly.

"I told you your dad had an *offer* from the Pittsburgh Pirates, while he was still in college, and that he turned it down because he wanted to graduate first. David, your dad was a good baseball player. He sent himself through college playing baseball. But he never played with the pros, and he never boxed a day in his life," I said sternly. "You can't just make up things like that. Then what happened?"

He started to cry.

"Billy said, 'You think your daddy's alive, but he's really dead. Your mom knows, but she won't tell you.'"

He was crying hard now.

"Is my daddy dead?" he wailed.

"I don't know, David. I've told you everything I know. I would never lie to you, and you mustn't lie either," I said. I knew I had to punish him, to make him stop fighting at school, to teach him to tell the truth. But I didn't want to. My heart was breaking for him, and for all of us.

I wanted to believe Leslie wasn't really aware of what was happening to Red. I knew it was hard for her to remember what her dad looked like. Her second-grade drawings of her family included no father. Ever since she could remember, her dad had been "missing in action." *How does a second-grader draw "missing in action"?* I knew she was deeply affected by his absence, but I wasn't sure that she thought much about what might be happening to him.

I was mistaken.

At Hoot and Laura Foote's dinner table, when she was six, she had stared wide-eyed at Hoot as he filled his plate.

"Do you always eat that much?" That was my Leslie, very direct and to the point.

Embarrassed, he said, yes, he usually did.

"My father never gets enough to eat," she said, matter-of-factly.

I wanted to insulate the children, to hide them from the real world. I wanted to be in the kitchen baking cookies when they came in from school, to build a fire on cold winter days, to smile and laugh and read bedtime stories.

But we were front page news. And we had to stay on the front page for God only knew how many more months and years. We had to talk about torture in a prison cell, and we had to match wits with bureaucrats and politicians in Hanoi and Washington. We had to make sure people kept talking about the POWs, so that when U.S. troops were withdrawn from a lost cause in Southeast Asia, the POWs came home too.

There was no turning back. We had to see that Red McDaniel was not forgotten. We had to keep our hard-won place on the front page.

9

The Tightrope

I kept the thin scrap of paper with Red's handwriting in the top drawer of the little blue chest on my side of the bed. Sometimes at night I would wake up from a sound sleep and bolt upright in bed. *I dreamed I got a letter from him,* I would say to myself.

Afraid to look, I would fumble in the dark for the drawer, reach in and search for Red's letter. When I found it, I would turn on the light and run my fingers over the flimsy white paper. It was real. It wasn't just a figment of my imagination. I would examine the postmark, "Hanoi, Vietnam, January 23, 1970," and think how he'd held this very same piece of paper in his hands not too many months ago. In spite of my decision not to read between the lines, I would read the fifty-one words again and again, trying to picture the man who wrote it, to guess about his physical condition, his frame of mind, his ability to endure, his will to survive.

Finally, when the little piece of tissue-like paper wore so thin that I was afraid it would tear if I handled it one more time, I decided to put it in our safety deposit box. *If Hanoi doesn't release him when the war ends, I'll bring out this letter in Red's own handwriting to prove to the world that he was alive all along, that he was in one of the POW camps from the beginning.* It belonged in our safety deposit box along with our other insurance policies. Because that is what it was, an insurance policy, proof to the world that Red McDaniel was a prisoner of war. It would serve as proof to U.S. negotiators with Hanoi, if negotiations ever took place; it was insurance against any attempt by his captors to hide him at the end of the war. Now we knew he was alive, and Hanoi knew that we knew.

And the United States government would have to delete the "presumed" in front of "captured" in the computer that stored the casualty list.

POW/MIA families had been advised that Hanoi had agreed to allow each POW one six-line letter a month. I followed the complicated instructions to a tee: use a six-line form identical to the one containing Red's letter to us, write only on the six lines, write only about health and family, mail only one letter each month.

In spite of Hanoi's supposed agreement, I was almost positive that our letters were not reaching Red, and occasionally I allowed one of the children to write the once-a-month six lines. Leslie was just learning to write, her repertoire of words that of a first-grader, when she laboriously printed her first letter to her dad.

"Dear Daddy," she wrote. "I hope you are having a nice time in Vietnam. We are having a very, very nice time here."

If he gets this one, I said to myself as I dropped Leslie's letter into the mail slot, *he won't get much news, but perhaps he'll get a good laugh.*

It seemed this new "writing privilege" was another result of the families' publicity campaign. The Hanoi government wanted the world to think the POWs were receiving "humane and lenient" treatment. They even went so far as to agree to allow each POW to receive one six-and-one-half pound package every other month. *They are really hung up on the number six*, I thought. *Six-line letters, six-pound packages.*

The packages had to be routed through Moscow because the Soviets had somehow helped to get this agreement with Hanoi. We were allowed to send nonperishable food items, vitamins, and *pictures* of the man's family! I had my doubts. I couldn't visualize someone just handing Red a package of goodies from home. But perhaps they would give him the pictures.

Assembling the six-and-one-half pounds became my priority task. I would take the little box unsealed to the post office, put it on the scale, and add fraction-of-an-ounce items like little packets of sugar or one more snapshot, as many fractions as I could possibly squeeze into the weight limit. I would mail that package, go home, and begin that very same day to plan what I would send in the next one, two months later.

A picture is worth a thousand words, I thought. My snapshots were carefully composed to tell Red what we wanted him to know. When David started playing Little League baseball, we sent a picture of him in his uniform standing in front of our seven-year-old car that was still up and running, with the long-leaf pine Red had transplanted from North Carolina in the background. That one picture would tell him more than any six-line letter could possibly say. After we got the letter from Red, I gave even more thought to the letters and packages, on the outside chance that he might actually receive one. And I really worked on the snapshots, because I knew they would be of no use to a Vietnamese guard who might want to keep the food and other goodies for himself.

The caption the *Virginian Pilot* had written under our picture when Red's letter came, "The McDaniel Family Has New Hope," was certainly true. The letter gave us a reason to hope that Red would come home some day. But I no longer envied Janie and the other POW wives who had been receiving mail all along. Because now, instead of wondering whether Red was dead or alive, I could actually visualize him in his prison cell, waiting, wondering, and hurting. The man I loved was hurting, and I could do nothing to try to make the hurting go away.

I knew I would never have gotten the letter if I had obeyed the keep-silent rule. I would never know until I saw him again how Red would react to my decision to defy the admonition not to talk to the press. I was thankful that I had been hesitant about being so much in the public eye. It would have been a mistake to parade my sorrow earlier, while I was still in shock and unable to control my emotions. And I felt certain that the first months of Red's captivity had been the most critical ones for him in his effort to resist, to avoid making the propaganda statements that I knew would be so abhorrent to him. I was certain that he had been tortured severely in an effort to make him denounce the war and talk about his "humane and lenient" treatment. Anything I had said to the press would surely have been relayed to him, and the last thing he needed to hear was me crying on television. So, in that regard, the keep-silent rule had proven helpful. By the time the wives and families had decided to go public, we had been able to plan very carefully what we would say and how we would say it, always aware that we might put additional pressure on our husbands. We always tried to look good and appear to be positive and in control. Even now I wasn't certain that I was doing the right thing; I could only trust that God would let me know if what I was doing was harmful to Red, just as I had asked Him to do before my first speech in 1968.

I knew I had to keep talking about Red. Now I spoke to audiences about the Vietnamese's inhumane treatment of the American POWs they were holding, and about the fact that some men were still missing. Several POWs had accepted "early release" and had come home to tell about the unbelievable torture they had suffered. Their stories received a great deal of press, adding credibility to our publicity campaign. The families of the POW/MIAs now thought it might be possible to put enough pressure on Hanoi that they would agree to a Red Cross inspection of the camps. We thought we might stop the torture if we talked about it enough. And we knew we had to keep pressing for the names of the men who had not yet been acknowledged by the Hanoi government.

The informal "league of families" now had a coordinator in every state, and I became the coordinator for all the POW/MIA publicity in Virginia. Almost one hundred POW/MIA families lived in Virginia, concentrated in Tidewater and northern Virginia. In May of 1970, a month after Red's letter came, I flew to Washington once again, this time to meet with thirty other POW/MIA family members to formalize the league and establish it as a national organization. This ad hoc committee decided on the structure and bylaws of the National League of Families of American Prisoners and Missing in Southeast Asia. Now we were incorporated, and the League of Families had a Washington presence, with national headquarters. We had come a long way, accomplished a seemingly impossible task. A handful of housewives scattered across the country had begun a national campaign to make sure our men were not forgotten—by the people or the politicians.

Some of the most widely-covered stories in 1970 about POW/MIA wives concerned their trips to Paris and Vientienne to ask the North Vietnamese and the Pathet Lao, "Are we wives or widows?" Some families traveled to Stockholm and other foreign capitals to publicly request that the diplomats of governments friendly to Hanoi intercede on their husbands' behalf. The wives in our area decided to try something different: to send a delegation of private citizens representing the hundreds of thousands of people who lived in Norfolk and Virginia Beach to appeal to the North Vietnamese government.

"The North Vietnamese know the wives and families care; we need to demonstrate to them that the *American people* care," I said to the mayor of Virginia Beach. Jane Denton and I had come to his office to ask him to go to Paris and meet with the North Vietnamese diplomats on behalf of the missing men from Tidewater.

Without a moment's hesitation, Mayor Rhodes agreed to go. So did Norfolk's Mayor Martin; Ed Brandt, editor of the *Virginian Pilot*; and William Mitchell, vice-president of the student body at Old Dominion University.

A Virginia Beach businessman let us use a vacant pre-fab building on a grassy slope beside the Norfolk-Virginia Beach expressway, and we opened our headquarters with a big red and white banner reading, "Don't Let Them Be Forgotten!" Now we would have a place for our volunteers to work. We could combine our assorted POW/MIA files and mailing lists, and use our headquarters as a backdrop when we kicked off our big campaign to send the delegation to Paris.

Volunteers began to circulate petitions to the North Vietnamese and the National Liberation Front on Oct. 22, 1970, in shopping centers and grocery stores, in parking lots and on street corners. That day we launched "Operation We Care" in front of our new headquarters, with our four-man delegation and all the local press in attendance. I introduced the members of the delegation and thanked them for being willing to "travel to Paris on behalf of the twenty-one missing men from Norfolk and Virginia Beach."

"The North Vietnamese cannot ignore the voices of all the people from our two cities. We must make them understand that Americans care about the twenty-one men from Tidewater and the other 1,500 sons of America who are missing—and that the American people would be equally concerned about only five men, or *only one* man," I concluded, as the TV cameras whirred.

In November, the world press covered the delegation's arrival on the street in front of the North Vietnamese Embassy in Paris. Several huge canvas mailbags stuffed with the petitions signed by the people of Tidewater were stacked on the sidewalk beside them. More importantly, the people of Tidewater were now very familiar with the missing men and our campaign, and we knew they would not let our men be forgotten.

Similar media events were taking place all over the country in front of similar makeshift headquarters. People were coming up with all kinds of creative ideas and publicity stunts. Bamboo cages, much like the ones holding American POWs of the Viet Cong in South Vietnam, appeared in shopping centers. A photograph of a POW in a solitary cell in Hanoi appeared on donated billboard space in major cities. POW/MIA wives appeared in ads distributed by the National Ad Council to major newspapers and magazines. One of the ads was a photograph of me standing in front of Red's picture and a picture of Mike, David, and Leslie, asking why Hanoi wouldn't let my POW husband write to me. I had agreed to do the ad, but every time I saw it in a newspaper or magazine, my heart would stop. It was a long way from "stay home and take care of the kids." I would stare at my picture, hoping my face didn't betray the anxiety and fatigue I was feeling, in case the Vietnamese should show it to Red. I was sure that they would. Once again, I was glad I had not been so public in the early days to create added pressure on Red. Now, however, I knew it was necessary.

Some college students in California came up with the idea of the POW bracelet which so captured the imagination of grassroots America. The narrow aluminum band bearing the name and date of casualty of a missing man was to be worn until the man returned. When I first heard the POW bracelet idea, I didn't like it. It didn't fit in with our dignified, white-gloves-and-pearls approach. But the bracelet turned out to be the one idea that caught on across the country. By the time we were standing on street corners with petitions, and building bamboo cages in shopping centers, the bracelet had become one of our most effective weapons.

I presented a bracelet stamped with Red's name to our local congressman, Representative Bill Whitehurst, who wore it faithfully. Every year on May 19, the anniversary of Red's shoot-down, a beautiful bouquet of flowers would arrive from Congressman Whitehurst with his note promising to make sure that any peace agreement would include the return of American POWs.

When he's sitting at his desk in Washington, when he's on the House floor, everywhere he goes, this congressman sees the name of my POW husband. I could tell from the thousands of letters I received from other people who were wearing the thin silver bands bearing Red's name that the bracelets had made the POWs real to grassroots America. The American people were now emotionally involved in our cause.

I knew we had made our men important to the politicians in Washington, as well. I also knew the families would continue to walk a tightrope until the war ended. Our public thrust had to be pressure on the Hanoi government. We were, for the most part, military wives loyal to the losing cause in Vietnam. Our men were military men; they followed orders; they didn't ask questions. We were military wives; our men expected us to be loyal too. At the same time, we were becoming a political force that the politicians had to take seriously. Somehow we had to focus public attention on Hanoi and maintain the pressure on Washington, all the while remaining loyal to the "cause" and to our husbands' sense of duty.

Now national policy was to get U.S. troops out of Southeast Asia and cut our losses. The government had decided not to win the war. The "secret plan to end the war" Richard Nixon talked about in his first presidential campaign turned out to be something called "Vietnamization." United States troops would gradually withdraw from Southeast Asia, turning the war over to the Vietnamese themselves. It sounded good. But there was a hitch.

How do you *gradually withdraw* American POWs from their prison cells?

The task of the National League of Families now was to publicly pressure Hanoi while privately pressuring Washington, a hard balance to maintain and the tightrope we had to walk.

POW/MIA families were on the front pages of the nation's newspapers. Most of us had learned enough about politics by this time to know that the threat of what we might do was the lever we needed to make sure our men were not left behind as U.S. troops were withdrawn.

I suspected that the bureaucrats charged with "handling" the POW wives were hard-pressed to know what to do with us as the war slowly wound down. Our tightrope grew ever narrower as American troops gradually trickled home from Southeast Asia.

I had received seven more of the six-line letters in 1970. They all said about the same thing, always beginning with "My health is good." I decided that was what Red had to say to get the Hanoi government to mail the letters. In the letter he wrote in April 1970, he asked us to send pictures and vitamins and said he hoped to get a letter soon. I assumed from that letter that some of the men were, in fact, receiving the packages. But Red evidently had not received any of the items I had sent in my packages, and he had not received any of the letters I had mailed through the years. However, in his next letter, written in June, he thanked us for the pictures and vitamins and the pair of red socks we had enclosed in the package we sent him for Christmas in 1969. It was obvious that the POWs' treatment had improved; at least they were receiving mail and some of the items from the packages.

But Red's October letter, which arrived just before Christmas, broke my heart. The handwriting was shaky and he asked us to write to him. "I had hoped to be home for Christmas this year," he wrote, "but I am well. Merry Christmas."

In 1971 we received only four letters, and the letters contained questions that let us know he wasn't receiving our letters. However, he talked about pictures and a jar of honey so we assumed he was receiving some of the items we were including in the bi-monthly packages. In one of the letters he wrote in 1971, he said, "I hope our dog Kelly is okay; he wasn't in any of the pictures." Kelly was his navigator and this letter let us know he had no information about what had happened to him after they bailed out over North Vietnam four years ago. Kelly's parents had never heard from him but they were sure he was in one of the camps, and I had prayed that Red would be able to tell us about Kelly in some way. *It must be awful for him, not knowing what happened to Kelly*, I thought. *And how is this going to affect Kelly's parents?* I knew I had to share the letter with the Navy so they could relay what Red had said to Mr. and Mrs. Patterson.

I worried that receiving less mail from Red was somehow connected to my POW/MIA activities. Had they shown him some of my TV interviews or singled him out for more pressure because of some of the public statements I was making? But I knew I had to shake those feelings off; we had no choice but to press on. It was a chance I had to take.

In 1972, Red's letters sounded more upbeat, and we received them more often. He had received a jar of peanut butter and some vitamins, and he mentioned pictures in every letter. But he wasn't getting my letters. "Continue answering my questions," he wrote. "I hope to receive an answer some day." I was surprised the Vietnamese let that one through. In another letter, he said, "I remain well but it seems like an eternity."

We received a total of twenty-seven letters in the six years of Red's captivity, all of them in the last three years. Every letter was carefully scrutinized. I couldn't help trying to read between the lines, trying to determine his physical condition and his frame of mind. We tried to analyze every word, to find a hidden meaning, to guess at what was actually happening to him. What message was he really trying to send us?

Sometimes the references he made to other people were puzzling. While "our dog Kelly" was obviously his navigator, I wondered why, in one of the last letters we received, he mentioned "Syl."

"I'm proud of you; you were doing so well during Syl's visit last fall," he wrote in November 1972. We knew only one person named Syl. Syl and Shirley Chumley were dear Navy friends who were now stationed at NAS Albany in Georgia.

Syl had flown many missions over North Vietnam. His A-4 Skyhawk had been hit on one of the sorties, but he was able to fly his crippled aircraft to the very edge of the Gulf of Tonkin, where he bailed out and swam out to sea under heavy gunfire before being dramatically picked up by an Air Force rescue plane. I knew his combat tour was over and that he was now on "shore duty," so Red couldn't be referring to him. But Syl had been in Norfolk for a few days in late 1971, and I had gone out to dinner with him and one of his Navy flyer friends. Who? I couldn't remember Syl's friend's name. Could Red be referring to Syl's friend? Shirley would know. I ran to the telephone and dialed the Chumleys' Georgia number.

"Shirley, I just got a very interesting letter from Red," I said to my good friend.

"Oh, Dorothy, that's great? How is he?" Shirley was always so concerned about us. She had given a lot of hours to "Operation We Care" when Syl was stationed at the Armed Forces Staff College in Norfolk, and she and Syl had often included the children and me in their family's holiday celebrations. We had many friends who invited us into their homes and included us in their parties, but very few of them ever invited us to their private family occasions. So the Chumleys were very special to me.

"Shirley, it's hard to tell how he really is," I told her on the phone. "Time is hanging heavy for him; I can tell that from some of the things he does say. But listen to this: 'You were doing so well during Syl's visit last fall.' "

Shirley hesitated for a moment.

"Last fall? Syl visited you last fall, remember?" She paused, thinking, then suddenly she said excitedly, "Oh, Dorothy, he's talking about Ron Polfer! Ron was with Syl and met you and the children. Ron's plane went down several months ago and Ron is still listed as missing in action! His wife Veda lives just a few blocks from here. She hasn't heard a word since Ron's plane went down. I need to run over there and tell her right now!"

"Wait, Shirley. Red doesn't actually give Ron's name," I cautioned. "Perhaps we should check with the Navy first."

"But what else could it be?" Shirley asked. "Veda'll want to know it right away. Wouldn't you want to know it now, if you were in her place?"

"Yes, I would. You're right, Shirley. Go tell her; I'll tell the Navy," I replied.

I knew Shirley was right about telling Veda. Even though Red hadn't actually said "Ron" or "Polfer," it had to be a reference to him. The POW/MIA wives were always being cautioned about what the services called "false hope," but I knew from my own experience that false hope was better than no hope. The wives I knew wanted to know whatever there was to know. With God's help, we were handling many things: pain, anxiety, nightmares, the responsibilities of homes and families, decisions about the POW/MIA campaigns. We could surely handle a little false hope.

I searched my memory, trying to recall every detail of my evening with Syl and Ron. I was so glad Ron had met Mike, David, and Leslie and could tell Red about them. I remembered that Ron had asked me a lot of questions about my work with the National League of Families. Now he could tell Red about that, too, and about all the American people who were wearing the POW bracelets and how the POW/MIA effort was making a difference in POW/MIA policy. I hoped that I had given Ron the impression that I was upbeat and optimistic, although I wasn't always.

"You were doing well during Syl's visit." *Oh, thank you, Ron, for telling him that.*

Since I was pretty sure Red wasn't getting my letters, I knew he would be desperate for word from home. I had been aware since the beginning that some of the flyers we knew might eventually end up with Red in the Hanoi Hilton, and that was one reason I still attended some of the squadron parties. In case any of these men should, God forbid, find themselves where Red was, I wanted them to tell him the children and I were okay. But that thought had not entered my mind during my visit with Syl and Ron. What a roundabout way for Red to hear from us! And what a roundabout way for Veda to find out about Ron. *Thank you, God.*

Just before Christmas, 1972, Red wrote, "I'm fine and in good spirits, happy about possible return home soon. Look forward to seeing you soon but if not will continue to find hope. Merry Christmas!"

I hoped he was right. My own hope was dwindling. It seemed to me in 1972 that the war would go on forever; there was no end in sight, in my opinion.

In May of 1972, my mother came to Virginia Beach to stay with Mike, David, and Leslie while I attended yet another National League of Families meeting in Washington. I didn't want to go this time. I was worn out. I was out of energy and I was out of ideas.

But my mother wouldn't let me give up.

"You can't quit now. Red's counting on you," she reminded me.

I had heard that Dr. Henry Kissinger, the President's National Security Advisor, might address our meeting. I hoped that I would have the chance to pose a question to him. I worked very hard to phrase it.

"Dr. Kissinger," I would say. "After working very hard for the past three years to build good press contacts and to arouse public concern for our men, I now find myself avoiding the press and the public because I am reluctant to express my strong criticism of the president's policy for ending the war. Would it be fair to say that the administration is now making an attempt to condition the American people for the very real probability that, although the troop level will be low enough to defuse the war issue by election day, our prisoners of war will not be home by then?

"The president now speaks of a 'residual force' remaining in Southeast Asia indefinitely. To say a residual force will remain after 1972 as an incentive for a POW release sounds less like a positive plan for the return of our prisoners and more like an excuse for the residual force."

I decided to end my question there and not include the rest of what I wanted to say to him.

"I intend to do everything in my power to see that the war in Vietnam is indeed an issue in this year's election so long as one more American is being asked to die and so long as one prisoner of war remains in his prison cell!"

In Washington, I once again heard the same reassuring words from the politicians. Once again, I heard how brave I was, how proud I should be of my husband, and how everybody was still "doing everything we can." I wondered how, after all these years, they could still be using that exact same phrase. Dr. Kissinger did not come to the meeting, so I didn't have the chance to ask my carefully constructed question. *It's probably just as well. I don't want to make a fool of myself. I'm not even sure I'm still thinking straight, at this point. And it probably wouldn't do any good, anyway.*

The meeting was a melee, with families shouting at one another, venting their frustration on people who were suffering just as they were. Those who supported the president questioned the patriotism and integrity of those who didn't. Those who didn't support the president accused those who did of not really caring about the men, of being caught up in the "Rose Garden scene," the visits with the president and his top advisors. I knew there was nothing more this organization could do for Red, and I was heartsick.

I was sitting next to Jane Denton at Friday night's banquet.

"Jane, I think the man across the table is from the Secret Service," I whispered. "What do you think?"

Jane nodded.

"I think you're right. There's one at every table," she whispered back.

They're going to send the president to our dinner, I thought, startled.

"Ladies and gentlemen, the president of the United States!" a voice boomed from the podium.

All around me, the wives and families of America's missing men jumped to their feet, cheering wildly.

It worked again, I thought cynically, glued to my seat.

President Nixon, both hands held aloft, fingers forming his famous "V for Victory" sign, praised us for our loyalty and asked us to "keep the faith."

I could not applaud him. I knew that I should. After all, he was the president of the United States. Not only that, but the man from the Secret Service was watching me, conspicuously sitting there, hands clenched in my lap.

I was sure the president was genuinely concerned about the POWs. But all I could hear were the bureaucrats behind the scenes.

"Keep them happy at any cost," they were saying.*

We wanted so much to believe. We wanted to have faith that our country would not abandon our men. We wanted to think that the president of the United States was working night and day to bring them home. That's what he said. And he *was* the president of the United States. He had come down from the White House to reassure us, to remind us to "keep the faith." But the words didn't ring true anymore. And the families' reaction frightened me. How could we keep the pressure on if we were so easily placated?

---

*Years later, a reporter brought me memoranda from the Nixon administration which confirmed my suspicions that presidential aides were given the job of administering "PR therapy" to POW/MIA wives to keep us "in line." (See appendix A.)

This is my last trip to Washington, I decided. *I rest my case. I'll go home and just try to be a good mother. I'll stay off the front page and out of the fray and try to undo some of the damage this whole thing has done to my children.*

I had my hands full with my two now-teen-age sons and Leslie, who would soon be a teen-ager herself. Mike was fifteen, rebellious, and caught up in the culture of the sixties, with hair down to his shoulders. David, thirteen, had decided to fight the battles by letting his hair grow long, too, and talking back to his teachers. Leslie was trying to grow up too fast, to be a teen-ager right now. She no longer cried when something hurt, and I could only guess at what was behind those knowing blue eyes.

They needed me. They needed me to be a mother—and a father, too. I couldn't be their father, but I could be a good mother, if it wasn't too late. Time was passing. They would soon be grown.

When I got home from the Washington meeting, they were all sitting at the kitchen table—Mike, Dave, Leslie, and my mother. My mother was ladling bright red spaghetti sauce over the steaming hot noodles on their plates.

Mike looked up at me.

"How'd it go, Mom? Did you accomplish anything? Or is it all just a waste of time?" He asked bitterly.

"Who knows, Mike? We have to keep trying, though, don't we?" I answered him, unconvinced in my own heart.

"Yeah, I guess," he said. I could see he was about to cry.

David stared at me.

"I don't know how we can keep trying," he said angrily. "What else is there we can do? Tell me that."

"I can't, David." I wanted to cry, too. "I don't know what else to do."

Leslie was studying the spaghetti on her plate, twirling the noodles around and around with her fork.

"We can pray," my mother said, "we have to keep praying."

"We've *been* praying," David said through clenched teeth. "We've been praying for five years, and nothing's happened."

"A lot has happened, David," my mother said quietly. "You got the letter you prayed for."

"Yeah, well, that was more than two years ago. Then we got a few more. But we haven't had one for a long time now." He slammed his napkin down on the table.

I leaned against the door and looked at Red's three children who had grown up without him, who were struggling, like he was, to survive.

Mike got up and left the room. *He'll want to be alone,* I knew. *He doesn't think a fifteen-year-old should cry.* My mother put her arm around Dave's shoulders.

"God will take care of your dad, David," she said.

"I know," he mumbled, looking down at his plate.

I sat down at Mike's place.

"Eat your spaghetti, Leslie," I said. Methodically, she began putting the spaghetti into her mouth, one strand at a time.

"May I be excused?" David asked defiantly.

"Yes," I replied testily. "You, too, Leslie."

When they had left the room, I turned to my mother and said wearily, "They'll be grown before they see their father again. . . if they ever do see him again."

I slipped out to the front steps, sat down on the bricks, and hugged my knees. *He that dwelleth in the secret place of the Most High shall abide under the shadow of the Almighty. Oh, God, where is your shadow?*

But there was no answer.

10

It's Over!

During the weeks and months that followed, I tried to put
Red out of my mind. I knew there was nothing more I
could do for him. I had tried to keep him on the front page, but
now I decided it was useless. Only the president could bring him
home, and all the president seemed to be interested in was his reelection campaign—and how to keep the POW wives in line until
after election day.

Congressman Whitehurst, the Republican congressman from
Tidewater who wore Red's POW bracelet, had withdrawn his support of the Nixon administration's policy of gradual withdrawal
and was now urging a negotiated settlement: withdrawal condi-
tioned on the release of the American POWs. Just before the election, Henry Kissinger announced, "Peace is at hand." He didn't
elaborate, and I decided it was just another election day ploy. By
Christmas B-52 bombers were flying raids over Hanoi. I should
have recognized that as the beginning of the end, but I didn't. *Here
we go again*, I thought.

I wanted so much to see democracy prevail in South Vietnam.
Selfishly, I wanted it almost more for Red than for the South Vietnamese people. I thought the ultimate tragedy would be for Red to
come home and know that the sacrifice of six years of his life, the
torture and the deprivation he had gone through, had all been for
nothing. But I knew the United States had decided long ago not

to win the war. We had never fought to win, and we certainly weren't about to begin now. By the end of 1972, there was practically no support among the American people for a continuing presence in Southeast Asia, and I didn't believe South Vietnam could survive without a residual American force. Just as I myself was defeated, so was my country.

However, as I looked back over the almost six years since Red was shot down, I realized that his first letter, received in March 1970, had come just as I was beginning to lose hope that we'd ever hear from him. Did I dare trust that he'd come home just as I was losing my hope that we'd ever see him again?

God's timing is perfect. Where had I heard that? Could it possibly be true? If so, then Red would be home soon. I knew I was sinking into despair, and I knew I couldn't afford the luxury; the children needed me too much. But I didn't want to get my hopes up, only to have them come crashing down around me. That would finish me; I knew it would.

Then, suddenly, without warning, it was over.

The president's voice was unsteady as he announced the peace agreement made between the United States and the North Vietnamese in Paris on Jan. 27, 1973.

"And all American prisoners of war will be released within the next sixty days."

It was really over!

Oh, God, your timing was perfect. Thank you; oh, thank you, I whispered audibly, feeling faint.

I was sitting on our old brown tweed sofa in front of the television, surrounded by six members of my bridge club. I realized that Marian Robertson had disappeared. Moments later, she stood in the doorway, holding a two-dollar bottle of Cold Duck, hastily purchased at the corner convenience store. Alice Myers was reaching for the champagne glasses, which I noticed, with some embarassment, were covered with seven years' worth of dust. Marian poured the wine, and the eight of us toasted the end of the Vietnam War.

Perhaps I had misjudged this president. Perhaps this had been the plan all along. Perhaps the political threat posed by the POW/MIA families had helped prompt the decision to send the B-52 bombers into North Vietnam just before Christmas of 1972, bringing about this negotiated settlement. Perhaps I would never know.

Anyway, it made no difference now.

Red was coming home!

And pandemonium reigned at our house. The telephone rang incessantly. Flowers from friends, and also from strangers, poured in the front door. Mail came in baskets, letters from people we knew, and from people we didn't know who had worn the slim, silver bracelets inscribed with Red's name.

"What we are doing may not bring your father home," I had once said to Mike. "But when he does come home, people are going to know who he is!"

The American people had responded magnanimously to the families' appeals on behalf of our husbands and sons. To them, the POWs were heroes. They had served their country well, and they had endured. For as many as nine years in some cases, they had stood fast, and now they were coming home to freedom, to receive the recognition and praise of their countrymen.

It is the people, the ordinary people from all across this land who are bringing them home, I thought.

The people of Tidewater could barely contain their excitement. I was astounded by the kindness of friends and strangers alike. Ruth Cunningham, a good friend and neighbor who belonged to my church, invited all my friends to a surprise "bridal shower" for me in her home, and the women "showered" me with new lingerie. One little white-haired lady, a wicked gleam in her eye, presented me with a very sexy red shortie nightgown. I took our eight-year-old car in for cleaning and servicing, and it was returned to me with a new paint job, the front seat filled with flowers. A local furniture store delivered a new recliner chair as a "Welcome Home" present. A woman I didn't know called to say she was keeping a scrapbook of press clippings for us so we "wouldn't have to bother." Another woman baked a beautiful cake decorated with an American flag and the inscription, "Happiness is POWs Coming Home!" and had it delivered to us.

The military services frantically completed elaborate preparations for Operation Homecoming. This flawless plan for the return and rehabilitation of men who had been incarcerated for years, isolated, starved, and beaten, was carried out to the most minute detail.

Red carpet was installed on the seventh floor of the Portsmouth (Virginia) Naval Hospital and other military hospitals selected as sites for caring for the returning POWs. A military officer of similar rank and background was recruited as a volunteer to serve as an escort and aide to each man for as long as he was needed.

Commander Al Weseleskey was commanding officer of a helicopter squadron which had flown combat sorties in South Vietnam.

"I've been assigned to be Red's aide," Wes told me when he introduced himself on the telephone a few days after the cease-fire. "He'll be released in the second group, so we can expect him in late February.

"I'd like to meet you and learn as much about you and Red as I can," he continued, and I invited him to come over right away.

It turned out that Wes already knew quite a bit about us. He had done his homework, familiarizing himself with Red's background and with my involvement with the POW/MIA public awareness effort. He was the father of four, a real family man, and I could tell he was excited about the assignment he had volunteered for, to help Red with his readjustment to freedom.

No doubt Wes assumed that I already knew what the Navy had told him, that Red McDaniel was one of the most brutally tortured of all the POWs. We were talking about what Red might want to do with his future, when Wes dropped a bombshell.

"Well, you know, Red may want to take some time off to write about his experiences. They'll give him a sabbatical, if he wants it."

My eyes widened.

"Why would he want to do that?"

Wes hesitated.

"His experience was unique," he said cautiously. And he let it go at that.

I was shaking when Wes left.

What had they done to the strong, vigorous man I loved? What would he be like when he returned?

The nightmare was over, wasn't it?

I had to push my fear into the back of my mind. There was work to do. I had my own frantic preparations to make. All the available space in Red's and my bedroom had been taken over by my POW/MIA files. Stacks of newspaper clippings, bulky copies of the *Congressional Record*, letters from Washington, letters from people who had worn the POW bracelet with Red's name on it, and copies of my speeches lined the walls. Most of the drawers and both closets were full of paper, six years' worth of my amateur efforts to bring Red home.

My first inclination was to throw it all away, to put it all behind me, to wipe it from sight and from memory. But then I hesitated. *Red will want to see some of this,* I thought. *He's not going to believe the magnitude of the effort made by so many people for him and a small number of other American POWs. He may need it. It will reaffirm his faith in the American people.*

It took several days to sort it all out. The children helped me select the papers we thought would mean the most to Red, and we stored as many as we could fit into an old Navy footlocker in the attic. Then Mike, Dave, Leslie, and I bundled up the rest and built a big bonfire in the backyard, ignoring fire regulations, to celebrate "the end of Mom's public life." One piece at a time, we tore the stacks of paper into shreds and stoked the fire, watching the hard memories burn away.

I knew the children shared my apprehension. Who was this man who was coming back into our lives? Mike, especially, was worried. I knew he was wondering if his dad would like him the way he was, and how much Red had changed. What would their dad be like? I could see that all three of them were trying to prepare themselves for seeing him again.

We were sitting around the kitchen table after dinner a few nights before Red was to be released, and Mike and Dave started talking about some of the good times they had had with Red when they were younger. I was amazed that they remembered so many details about things that had happened so long ago.

"Remember when Dad chased the grizzly bear with a baseball bat while Mom was screaming at him to get back in the tent?" Mike asked, grinning broadly.

"What about the time that we caught that toadfish off the pier in Brunswick?" Dave asked. "Remember how Daddy used to put a fish on my line when I wasn't looking, so I would think I caught one?"

Mike laughed.

"I remember how you used to lean your pole against the rail and run around looking through the holes in the pier. I was always afraid you were going to fall in."

Leslie was pensive, searching for some small memory of her dad.

"I think I remember him," she said, with a wistful look in her eyes. "Did he wear a tan suit and swing me up on his shoulders when he came in the front door?"

I was trying, too, but I could not remember his face.

So much was happening, and happening so fast, that I only gave the baskets of mail a cursory glance. I rifled through the cards and letters looking for those from personal friends and put the others aside, hoping to find the time to read them when things settled down. So it was several days after it arrived that I noticed the small white envelope postmarked in the Philippines. The return address indicated that the letter was from Colonel James Lamar in Little Rock, Arkansas. But the back of the envelope, which I had not seen before, said "American National Red Cross." I examined the envelope more carefully and saw that it was mailed by the Air Force Postal Service at Clark Air Force Base in the Philippines. I tore open the envelope. There was a note from Colonel Lamar dated February 13, 1973:

Dear Mrs. McDaniel,

Red asked me to bring this letter out and mail it to you. He is in good health, with no injuries that I know of, and his spirits are sky-high. For your information, as nearly as we (those who were released yesterday) were able to determine, Red is in the next group of 115 prisoners to be released. That should occur in two weeks. Goodbye and good luck!

Jim Lamar

Colonel Lamar's note was wrapped around a tiny scrap of red paper with Vietnamese lettering that looked like the wrapper from a pack of cigarettes. On the back of the thin paper Red had written the only real letter he wrote from Hanoi, the only one he had known would not be read by anyone but me. The tiny printed words were crammed on the small scrap of paper; I could hardly make them out.

My dearest family,

Standing on the threshold of freedom, I anxiously await with great anticipation my rebirth and the new beginning that lies ahead. There is so much to return to. I hope and pray that reentry into our great country will be as wonderful and successful as I have dreamed it would be for so many years. I have great expectations! You have done such a wonderful job and I am grateful and so in love with you. Perhaps soon, I can help you shoulder the great burden that has been yours for so long. The children are sure to present the most dramatic changes. I am extremely proud of them, too, and will surely be even more so seeing them in their teens. Though I have had so little news from home, the pictures have somewhat bridged the large time-span. I look forward to seeing Mike and David compete in sports and our beautiful daughter's dancing talent. Dorothy, I welcome the opportunity to seek the heights of happiness with you. I plan to dwell in the very depths of your warm and tender heart. I thank God daily for your love and devotion. You will see life begin at 40. Outwardly, I am well and feel that I have changed very little. I have tried very hard to return to you in the best possible health. These last days certainly are not the toughest but they are the longest. Stand tall until freedom arrives. We will have a great reunion soon.

I love you with all my heart,
Red.

My hands were shaking. Why had he said "outwardly" he was in good health? What was wrong with him? *Well, we'll soon find out.* "Life will begin at forty," he'd said. *He'll be home in March, in time for my fortieth birthday! Oh, my darling, yes, you will dwell in the depths of my heart. We will find the heights of happiness together, you and I. Nothing can possibly be wrong that you and I together cannot make right.*

I couldn't believe this wonderful love letter had lain in a basket of mail for several days—three or four, anyway—without my seeing it. *Oh, thank you, God. You're helping us get ready for him.*

The Navy notified us that Red would be released on the last Sunday in February. The Tuesday before, the North Vietnamese announced that the United States had violated the cease-fire. There would be no more POW releases, they said.

"Oh, God," I prayed, "don't let this be happening!"

And then I thought of Red. Surely he had been told he was going home. How much more could he take?

Sunday came. Nothing happened.

But two days later, the North Vietnamese, for no apparent reason, reversed their position. The second group of POWs, Red's group, would be released on Sunday, March 3. It had been a long, tense week for us. I was sure it had been for Red, too. Knowing other POWs had already been released must have given him hope. How had he felt when he heard his own release had been cancelled?

We held our breath. Could we count on it this time? David announced he wouldn't believe his dad was coming home until he saw him.

"I don't want to get my hopes up," he said.

Sunday finally came. We went to church, then came home and sat by the telephone. That night about 8:30, a Navy communications officer called from Oceana.

"Your husband's plane just entered free air space over the Gulf of Tonkin," he said. "He'll land at Clark Air Force Base in the Phillipines at 12:30 in the morning, our time. The three major networks will have live coverage of the landing."

Red was free! Four hours. In four hours, I would see him. And then I would actually talk to him, when he made the phone call from the Philippines Wes had told me to expect.

What would I say to him? What could possibly be good enough to say?

And what does he look like?

I couldn't think of anything to do except turn on the TV and wait for four hours. We all got our pillows and blankets, and Mike, David, Leslie, and I settled down in the family room for our last long vigil.

I looked at the clock on the mantle. Had it only been thirty minutes since they'd called me? Leslie had fallen asleep on the floor. Mike and Dave were watching "Bonanza."

I slipped out to the front steps, sat down on the familiar cold bricks, and hugged my knees. How many nights had I sat here like this? I had never seen the black sky so clear, or seen so many stars.

I heard the door close softly behind me.

"Are you okay, Mom?" Mike wanted to know.

"I think so. Are you?"

"Yeah, I guess. Do you think we'll recognize him? It's been a long time." He sat down on the bricks beside me.

"Well, Mike, you know, I have a hard time remembering what he looks like."

"Yeah, me too," he murmured. "Let's go in, Mom. It's cold out here. It'll be okay."

He's scared, too. He's excited, but he's also scared. I guess we all are.

Mike and I rubbed our hands in front of the fire, shivering. Dave was absorbed in a science-fiction movie. I looked at the clock again. Were those hands moving at all? Which channel should we watch? I sat down on the floor beside Leslie and pulled the blanket over her shoulders. The movie ended and WAVY–TV news ran some old clips of the POW wives' activities, reminding local viewers that four more POWs from Tidewater had been released in Hanoi and were on their way to the Philippines.

Finally, both hands on the clock were at twelve. I shook Leslie gently.

"Wake up, honey. It's almost time."

Almost twenty minutes went by. Then we saw it. The silvergray C-141 roaring in for a landing at Clark Air Force Base.

We watched the lumbering MEDEVAC plane roll to a stop on the brightly lit runway. The returning POWs started coming down the ramp in order of the date they were captured. Seven U.S. fighter-bombers had been lost over North Vietnam on May 19,

1967. Lieutenant Bill Metzger was flying one of them, and he came limping down the ramp now, grinning, and shook the extended hand of Admiral Noel Gaylor, who was standing on the tarmac.

"Welcome home, Lieutenant Metzger!" Admiral Gaylor boomed.

Long, skinny legs in baggy cotton trousers appeared in the doorway of the aircraft. The man's left hand straightened his belt buckle, a gesture I remembered from long ago.

"That's your dad!" I cried.

My tears hid his face. Tears held for six years kept me from seeing his stooped shoulders and the haunted look in his eyes. But I knew that I would know him.

The networks had promised to repeat the coverage the next day. It was now three o'clock in the morning. Mike, Dave, and Leslie were asleep on the floor in front of the TV. I stretched out on the sofa and pulled the blanket up, closing my eyes tightly. But sleep wouldn't come. I wanted to see his face.

Finally, it was morning. The reruns began. This time I knew exactly when to watch for him. Lieutenant Metzger again. Then the belt buckle. I could see him clearly as he bounded down the ramp and grasped Admiral Gaylor's big hand with both of his.

A wide grin broke his gaunt face.

I took a deep breath.

He's a whole man, I said to myself, profound relief sweeping over me.

Later, on the telephone, he was incredulous about the welcome he and the other returning POWs had received from the throng of people lining the runway at Clark.

"You haven't seen anything yet, Red. You're a celebrity! Hundreds of thousands of people, maybe even millions of people, have worked to bring you home. All of America is celebrating your freedom!" I told him.

"You look great, Red!" I added.

"I have some scars that don't show, Dorothy," he said slowly. And he began to tell me about the beatings and the rope torture and the electric shock treatments.

The gnawing in my stomach returned.

"I'll see you in a few days," he said.

11

Welcome Home!

Lieutenant Ralph Paulk stopped at the toll plaza on the way to Norfolk Regional Airport. His big hand was shaking as he moved the gearshift on the floorboard of his sleek red sports car.

This fresh-faced young Navy flyer had volunteered to serve as a part-time aide for me and the children during Operation Homecoming, all during his off-duty time. Three days after Red was released and was flown out of Vietnam, Ralph packed my two long-legged teen-age boys, my ten-year-old daughter and me into his tiny sports car and off we went to meet the C-9 aircraft that was bringing Red home to us.

A misty rain was falling. Heavy fog obscured the airport tower, as well as the huge red banner the congregation of the First Baptist Church in Virginia Beach had draped under the observation windows. "Welcome Home, Deacon Red!" the banner proclaimed.

Chartered buses had brought the entire membership of the church Red had served as deacon years ago to the airport to see him come home. Huddled under umbrellas and blankets, these friends who had prayed for Red and watched over his family for six years now stood in the pouring rain to welcome him. Thousands of people from Tidewater, people who had helped us in the publicity campaigns, waited, drenched in the downpour.

Mike, David, Leslie, and I were ushered into the airport's VIP room along with three other POW wives and their children. Admiral Ralph Cousins, commander in chief of the Atlantic Fleet, headed the contingent of high-ranking officers who greeted us. "Great Stone Face," Admiral Cousins was called by his men. Today "Great Stone Face" had tears in his eyes.

"We're weathered in," Admiral Cousins said to us. "The C-9 has been diverted to Oceana Naval Air Station. Your husbands will be driven to the Portsmouth Naval Hospital and we'll meet them there. Let's go!"

"But what about all those people out there in the rain?" I asked him.

"What about them?"

"Someone has to speak to them, to thank them for coming!" I said.

Admiral Cousins agreed with me and said he would explain the situation to the crowd after we left.

"No, I think we should go out there and speak to them ourselves," I argued. *I've come a long way*, I thought. *Here I am arguing with the commander in chief of the Atlantic Fleet!*

"We'll be late," he said.

"Admiral, those people standing out there in the rain helped us bring our husbands home. We couldn't have done it without them. We can't just drive off and leave them," I said.

Admiral Cousins relented.

"Go ahead. We'll wait for you," he said.

So Pat Fellowes, Charlotte Christian, Louise Brady, and I, wearing the big white orchids President Nixon had sent us, walked out of the airport into the rain, our twelve assorted almost-grown children trailing behind. The admirals went with us to tell the now very wet crowd that the men they had waited so long to see weren't landing after all.

Admiral Cousins explained that the C-9 couldn't land because of the fog and had been diverted to NAS Oceana. Then he invited the people to follow us to the hospital in Portsmouth. Next, each one of the wives said a few words.

I thanked the people for waiting so long in the rain and then I said, "This long-awaited day has come because you helped us. You have shared our sorrow. Thank you for also sharing our joy."

Darkness had fallen by the time our motorcade reached the hospital. The press and a few hardy friends had followed the official cars. Television klieg lights heightened the tension as Mike, Dave, Leslie, and I waited alongside Admiral Cousins on the rain-slick sidewalk in front of the hospital.

A shiny black Navy car pulled up to the curb. A long, lanky figure in dress khaki uniform leaped out of the back seat before the car came to a full stop.

Red was home!

He swept Leslie up with one long arm and threw the other one around me. Then he gathered all four of us into both arms and held on tightly, while the crowd cheered. I glanced down at David. His face was beaming, and he was standing on tiptoe, trying to look even taller than he was.

"Hi, Dad," he said with all the thirteen-year-old dignity he could muster.

"David, you're all grown up!" Red ruffled Dave's scraggly blond hair.

"You're eye-level with me!" he grinned at Mike as he crushed the president's orchid against his uniform, holding me close.

The press was closing in. Over Red's shoulder I could see tears streaming down the face of the anchorman for WAVY–TV News. This media friend had covered every public event the POW/MIA wives had staged for the past four years, even those which had little press value. You helped bring him home, too, my eyes told him silently.

Safely inside Red's seventh floor hospital room, all five of us started talking at once. Navy Chaplain Jim Rittenhouse helped us give thanks as a family reunited. In a circle, hands held tightly, the children and I knelt beside our returned POW on the new bright-red carpet.

"Thank you, God, for this day," Red prayed softly, lips trembling.

It was after midnight when Ralph took the children home. Hesitant at first, they had warmed to their stranger-father and had bombarded him with one question after another. And he, in turn, wanted to know everything they had done while he was away. Finally, I called a halt.

"Come on, kids. Everybody's tired," I said. "Lieutenant Paulk will bring you back tomorrow and then you can all have at each other again."

After they were gone, I got into one of the high hospital beds beside Red and put my arms around him. Underneath his now-thin torso, I could feel his strength and the once-familiar beat of his heart. His hands began to explore my body, very gently at first, and then with great urgency.

"It was worth it all for this moment," he whispered hoarsely, as the six years melted away.

12

Man with a Mission

"It's great to be home!"

Finally he was home, really home, at our little house nestled in the tall pine trees. Two weeks had passed since he took us in his arms in front of the Naval Hospital. Here he was, bigger than life itself, standing on the low brick steps in front of the door to our house, the steps that faced the trees and the winding street just beyond.

Shiny yellow ribbons, tied by my neighbors around each one of the twenty or so trees in our yard, gleamed in the blinding sunlight.

"Tie a yellow ribbon 'round the old oak tree if you still want me."

Out at the street, on our gray metal mailbox, someone had plastered one of the red plastic strips that were stuck on all the car bumpers in the neighborhood. The glossy white letters glistened:

"Welcome Home, Red McDaniel!"

A huge hand-lettered banner stretched from one side of the narrow street to the other, one end tied to the top of a telephone pole and the other to one of the tall trees:

"Welcome Home, Commander Eugene McDaniel!"

Television cameras rolled as the crowd of friends and neighbors filled the yard and spilled over into the surrounding lawns and on out into the street. Gangly teen-agers, in faded blue jeans and scruffy sneakers, and their younger brothers and sisters, some propped on their bikes and others leaning against the tree trunks, all cheered and clapped, grinning at Mike, David, Leslie, and me. My dad, his eyes swimming with tears, gripped one of my mother's arms tightly, while my sister Mary Joe clung to her other hand. Red's sister Bobbi and his brother Nathan each held one of their mother's trembling arms.

His face drawn and weary from all the excitement, Red stood beside me on the steps.

"It's really great to be home," he repeated to the crowd. "In Hanoi we clung to values we believed to be true. They were family, God, and the red, white, and blue."

Simple words, but somehow very profound.

The words told me that the bedrock beliefs deeply held for forty years of a man's life had not been shaken by six years of isolation and torture. Words that should have reassured me only added to a growing apprehension. Where would words like that take us?

I was tired. Tired from seven years of separation, six of them spent wondering if he would ever come home. Tired of long nights filled with torturous dreams and long days of dogged determination to make things better for three small children growing up without a father. Tired from too many trips to Washington and too many tense encounters with indifferent bureaucrats and blind politicians. The years of waiting had taken their toll.

You're supposed to be happy, excited, thankful, I said to the person hiding behind my smiling face.

But all I felt was a deep sense of relief. The nightmare was over. No longer would I have to wonder, is he still alive? Will we ever see him again? Will America ever get out of this quagmire called Vietnam? When we do bring the troops out, will we also get the POWs out? And will Red be one of them?

Here he was, standing on my (no, our!) front steps. Here he was, this patriot, this man I had loved so long ago, this familiar stranger who had come to live in our house again. The two weeks of decompression—letting go of some of the pent-up emotion, telling his horror story to Navy debriefers, eating all of his favorite foods and gaining a few pounds, looking through old newspapers and watching reruns on TV, being subjected to every physical and mental test known to medical science, and talking late into the night—were over.

I had moved into Red's hospital room to be with him twenty-four hours a day, to get to know him again, to make up for the six years, time that was lost to us forever. The hard hospital bed, he said, was too soft after six years of sleeping on a concrete slab, and for two weeks we slept on a blanket stretched out on the red-carpeted floor, arms wound tightly around each other. During the days, while he was with the doctors and the debriefers, I filled the hours helping volunteers answer the thousands of letters that poured in from people all over the world. Many people had sent him their POW bracelets, including a twelve-year-old boy whose bracelet had broken into three pieces and had been taped back together.

"I taped it to my arm and didn't take it off until I saw you on television," the boy had written. "I even got special permission from the coach to wear it when I played Little League baseball. You're not supposed to wear anything metal, but they let me wear your bracelet. Welcome Home, Commander McDaniel."

Ralph Paulk had brought Mike, Dave, and Leslie to the hospital every night for dinner in Red's room. Then we would all go downstairs to watch the World Series and Super Bowl games from the last six years, the children helping him catch up with what had happened in the sports world. We were beginning to be a family again.

Now the friends and neighbors and press people that had crowded around him on the front lawn were gone. The five of us joined our parents and brothers and sisters around the dining room table laden with food brought in by our generous, excited neighbors. There was so much to say, so many questions to ask, so much catching up to do. Our relatives would all be leaving within the next two or three days.

In the middle of lunch, I looked around for Red and didn't see him. I found him in the back yard, swinging in the rope hammock I had bought as a "Welcome Home" present. One hand behind his head, he was gazing into the patches of blue sky between the branches of the trees at each end of the hammock. I sat down beside him. He looked very tired and drained.

"Too much excitement?" I asked him.

"Too much color," he said. "The walls, the furniture, the pictures, the flowers, the food. I just can't handle all the color. My world has been gray for so long."

Suddenly I realized that both of us were in a daze from all that had happened in the few days he had been home. And I could see more hectic days ahead. There wouldn't be much privacy for us any time soon, I knew. Everyone wanted to see him. Speaking invitations from all over the country were arriving in the mail already. The press was clamoring for interviews.

It would be nice to just disappear from public view, I thought. But I realized the intense interest of the public was the price we had to pay for making his captivity front page news. And I knew he wouldn't even be here if our friends in the press hadn't helped us keep his name in the forefront while he was gone.

I was relieved to find that the Navy was flexible about when Red could leave the hospital for good and how soon he had to make decisions about his career plans for the future. He was chomping at the bit to get back into an airplane. But he was still officially attached to the hospital.

The Navy doctors had ordered a long and strict regimen of physical therapy for his spinal injuries and the broken arm he had sustained in the torture room, which had healed incorrectly. The therapy would require many trips back to the hospital in the months ahead. They could do little for the nerve damage in his arms and hands resulting from the rope torture; he would have to learn to live with the numbness. The meager POW diet of rice and pumpkin soup and a total lack of dental care had caused extensive damage to his teeth, and he would have to spend many long hours in the dentist's chair.

It was amazing to me to learn from him of the ways he and the other POWs had devised to care for themselves and for one another. Red's hands had dangled uselessly for several months following a severe and brutal beating in 1969, and his cellmate had massaged them for hours on end, slowly restoring the feeling and enabling him to regain limited use of his hands. When he'd had a tooth extracted without medication, he had discovered that nicotine would alleviate the ache where the tooth had been. He had poured his own urine into his ears to lessen the pain resulting from savage blows to his head.

The POWs had also made improvised devices to pass the long solitary hours and conquer the boredom that threatened to defeat them. They played chess with chessmen sculpted from bread dough, bridge with cards made from the stiff toilet paper, and they had fashioned juggling balls from wads of used bloody bandages. They had communicated with one another in codes tapped on the thick cinderblock walls. In solitary confinement, they played bridge through the walls. They'd even told jokes through the walls. The response of a slow, steady tap meant the joke was a dud; rapid, loud taps meant the joke was a winner.

The children and I listened wide-eyed to these stories, as we slowly learned to know him again. He was more hero than father to them, but I felt sure time would take care of that.

It was hard for Red not to rush ahead. There was so much he wanted to do. I had carefully prepared scrapbooks and photo albums, and the locker full of press clippings of my speeches and other POW/MIA activities was waiting in the attic. I thought he would want to catch up. But he had very little interest in looking back.

"That's all history," he said. "I want to live each day now, and look to the future. There's so much I want to do."

He talked with his children for hours at a time. Tolerant and patient with their shortcomings, he accepted them—long hair, ragged jeans and all. And, slowly, they learned to love him again. He was learning to be their dad again.

It was easier for Mike and Dave. But to Leslie, Red was a stranger who was trying to be a father, to take up where he left off. It wasn't possible. But Red was determined to make up for the time he had lost with his baby daughter.

The Ford Motor Company offered the use of a new car, any model, to each POW for the first year after he returned. Red decided to take Leslie with him to the Ford showroom to look at all the models available. She was very excited about his decision to let her select the car the family would use. When they returned, Red was driving a bright yellow Ford station wagon with a stereo tape deck, even though we didn't own any tapes. Leslie was strutting proudly alongside her dad as they came hand-in-hand up the front walk.

"I've always wanted our family to have a two-story house and a yellow station wagon," she said. "Now can we build a two-story house?"

She was really pleased that her new dad thought she was grown up enough to pick out the family car. It wasn't long before she decided she was old enough to do some other things, like shave her legs. When she asked me about it, I sent her to her dad for his opinion. Red told her she didn't need to shave her legs, that she was too young and would have to wait another year or two. So Leslie started working on him.

One day she came home from swim team practice at the community pool and confronted him in the garage, where he was trying to sort out his tools.

"Dad," she said confidentially, "I've really got a problem, and I need to talk to you right away."

Red closed his toolbox and leaned against the tool bench, giving his pretty, fair-skinned blonde daughter his full attention. He braced himself to hear the "serious problem," very pleased that she wanted to discuss it with him.

"Dad," she said, using all her feminine charms, "Everyone at the swimming pool says I look like a *hairy ape!* I really do need to shave my legs."

Later, Red came into the kitchen, scratching his head.

"I don't know how she does it," he said to me, "But my ten-year-old daughter can outsmart me every time. I hope you don't mind; I told her she could go ahead and shave her legs."

It was difficult for him to accept the boys' long hair and sloppy blue jeans, worn low on the hips. As a military man, he placed high value on short haircuts, shiny shoes, and trousers with sharp creases. He wanted his sons to look sharp. He had been away while hair styles slowly changed from crew cuts to shoulder-length and cordovans gave way to scuffed, dirty sneakers. The teen-age dress codes of the day were hard for him to tolerate. But he'd made a comment he had to stand by when he talked with Mike long distance from the Philippines the day he was released.

"I have long hair now, Dad," Mike had informed him hesitantly in their very first telephone conversation.

"Mike, I don't care if your hair grows down to your ankles," Red had responded impulsively. "It's your values that matter to me."

Later, I think he regretted having made such a rash statement, because every time he told Mike he needed a haircut, Mike would remind him of what he'd said about values.

But Red was determined to accept the children the way they were and to not try to make any major reforms too suddenly. I loved him even more for that. I wanted him to appreciate my struggle to handle things at home while he was away, and he did. I was especially sensitive to his opinions of his children, and any criticism of them I considered an insult to me.

My sensitivity about the children was one of the hurdles in the necessary readjustment process we faced. I didn't care what Red thought about anything else I had done while he was away, but I cared very much about his opinion of the children.

You were gone; I had to make decisions about family finances, investments, the car, the POW/MIA publicity campaigns, everything. You can second-guess me on any of that, if you like, but don't you dare criticize one of these children, no matter what you think!

He was puzzled by my overprotective attitude.

"You did a great job, Dorothy, much better than I would have expected you to do under those circumstances. Your ordeal was even worse than mine; I knew what was happening to me but you had to wonder," he said. "I always had confidence that you'd take care of things here. I didn't have to worry about that, and that relieved me of that anxiety and gave me what I needed to make it. I'm not criticizing. But they're my children, too, you know. Let me be their father."

Then I would feel guilty. *How can I do this to him after all he's been through?*

But as time passed, we all found our places again. Our home gradually became a refuge, a haven for each one of us. We learned to give and take and to be supportive, as we learned to love each other again and tried to regain the relationships we had lost.

*   *   *

The Navy granted Red's wish to fly the A-6A Intruder again, assigning him to Medium Attack Wing One at NAS Oceana. After his first orientation flight, he came home beaming.

"It felt great to get my hand on the throttle again," he said to me. "It all came back to me instantly. I can hold my own with those younger guys."

I knew how much he wanted to fly again. And I was thankful that he wasn't disabled, that he could still meet the stringent physical requirements for naval aviation. But I knew that this was going to mean more sea duty and more separations.

I wanted him home, with us. All the time. But I had to share him with the people from all over the country who wanted to hear him speak. He accepted as many of the invitations as he possibly could. People were eager to hear his story about his life as a POW, about how he had survived such incredible, unbearable torture. He had never done much public speaking, but he had a lot to say about patriotism and about faith.

His faith in God had brought him through his darkest hours in "Heartbreak Hotel" and the "Hanoi Hilton," and he had served as a chaplain of sorts for the other POWs in their rudimentary worship services. He believed his story could encourage people, and strengthen their faith.

The congregation of our own church had prayed for Red for six years, and they were spellbound as he told them how God had heard their prayers and had delivered him from the hands of his enemies.

"I want to share with you my faith in a great God," he began. "My faith has been severely tested. Sometimes it wavers still. But the God I believe in has never changed. He has always come through for me.

"The supreme test of my faith was six years in a communist prison cell. Six years is a long time to be in prison, to be away from your family, your friends, your country, and all that a man holds dear. And a communist prison camp is a desperate place to be.

"But God was able to turn that long and difficult period of my life into a tremendous learning time for me.

"I was shot down over North Vietnam on May 19, 1967, flying from the deck of USS *Enterprise*..."

Red described how he had parachuted into the top of the tree and fallen to the ground, crushing vertebrae in his lower spine. He told them about waiting all night for the rescue planes that never came, about dragging himself through the dense undergrowth in the futile attempt to locate Kelly.

"I prayed for rescue," he said. "I reminded God that I was a good churchman. Surely I deserved a better fate than this.

"'Why me, God,' I asked. 'Why me?'"

He told the story of his capture, the painful bumpy ride to Hanoi, and a little about the terrible torture.

"The torture turned out to be worse than I anticipated. Tightly-drawn ropes around both wrists and both ankles pulled my arms and legs backward against my back and lifted me off the floor. Hanging from a rafter in this contorted position, I felt my body bend in ways it isn't intended to bend. Mercifully, I slipped into and out of consciousness.

"What seemed to be three or four days later, they threw my bruised and battered body into a bare dirty cell. In the dim light, I saw the hollow eyes of another American. Raw open wounds covered his emaciated, naked frame. Lieutenant Bill Metzger grinned up at me. And I immediately changed my 'Why me?' question to 'Why not me?' One of the few verses of scripture I had committed to memory came to me. It was written by the apostle Paul, who knew how it feels to be locked away in a prison.

"'For we know that all things work together for good to those who love God, to them who are called according to His purpose.'

"Did God have a purpose for me here, in the Hanoi Hilton? Was his purpose for me to pick Bill Metzger up off the floor and tend his wounds? Was that one of the reasons I was here, in this dirty, gray prison?"

This congregation of believers who had shared their love with my family and me as they prayed for Red's safety listened intently as he told them how God had given him strength during the endless days and nights of confinement, deprivation, and sessions of barbaric torture. He ended his speech with another reference to St. Paul's letter to the Romans.

"'Who shall separate us from the love of Christ? Shall tribulation, or distress, or persecution, or famine, or nakedness, or sword?'

"That list is not just a list in a book," Red said. "I have experienced every one of those things. But Paul goes on to answer his own question:

"'For I am persuaded that neither death, nor life, nor angels, nor principalities, nor powers, nor things present, nor things to come, nor height, nor depth, nor any other creature, shall be able to separate us from the love of God, which is in Christ Jesus our Lord.'*

"I, too, am now persuaded of the power of God's love. And I believe, as I continue to learn and grow, God's purpose for me will become even clearer. I pray that I will be found faithful."

Seated in the pew with Mike, David, and Leslie, I remembered my long nights on the front steps. *God, your shadow did reach all the way to Vietnam.*

I thought about what Red had said to our neighbors assembled to welcome him home—about God, and about country. The purpose God had for Red was already becoming clear to me.

One thing was especially clear. Our future would not include a little rose-covered cottage where we could just rest and recover from the trauma we had all endured. The children and I would have to share this man. Because the man standing in the pulpit of the First Baptist Church that Sunday morning was clearly a man with a mission.

---

*Romans 8:28, 35, 38–39.

13

Leader of Men

In one of the sporadic letters we had received from Red while he was in the Hanoi Hilton, he had asked a question that had puzzled me.

"Have you had an occasion to have a 'wetting down' party by the new pool?" he had written.

I knew he was referring to the community swimming pool that had been under construction in our subdivision when he left for Vietnam. I also knew a wetting down party was the Navy's traditional way of celebrating an officer's promotion to a new rank. I should have been able to make the connection between the two, but I didn't.

Red's old squadron mate, Hoot Foote, interpreted the letter for me.

"He wants to know if he made commander," Hoot said when he read it.

"Why would he care about that?" I wanted to know.

"If you have to ask that, you don't know your husband very well!" Hoot laughed.

Red was promoted to the rank of commander while he was away. Soon after he came home, because of his outstanding record in Vietnam, he was "early-selected" for the rank of captain. Shiny new captain's stripes were added to his uniform along with rows of medals and decorations, including the Navy Cross, two Silver

Stars, the Distinguished Flying Cross and two Purple Heart medals for the wounds he received in the torture room. His new captain's stripes made him eligible for ship command. He had been home two years when he was selected to command the supply ship USS *Niagara Falls*, home-ported in Alameda, California.

"I'm not going!" announced Mike, now in his senior year of high school.

"You're a part of this family, and this family is going," Red informed him, firmly. "It'll be tough for you, but you can handle it."

He'd come a long way with his children. Now he could lay down the law, as a father they loved and respected. Mike had been chosen to represent his high school at Boys' State at the end of his junior year. We decided he could stay behind for that, and then join us in time for fall football practice at his new high school and complete his senior year in California.

Dave and Leslie were also reluctant to be uprooted, to leave their friends and the home where they were finally feeling secure. And I was a little resentful. My own circle of friends had expanded beyond the Navy into the civilian community while Red was gone, and I didn't want to say goodbye to the people who had given of themselves so generously when I had needed them.

There are plenty of ships right here in Norfolk. Why does it have to be California? Command at sea would also mean another separation for us.

But Red was excited. And the rest of us soon caught his excitement. *It will be interesting to see what life holds for our family next. We can drive from Virginia to California and see parts of the country we haven't seen before. And I can learn how to be a Navy wife again.*

The *Niagara Falls* crew were skeptical of their new skipper. He had never had a command. He was an aviator; what did he know about handling a ship? He had been locked up in a POW cell for six years. How could he possibly command their ship?

Niagara Falls was scheduled for a seven-month deployment to the western Pacific just one week after Red assumed command. The ship had to sail from the Oakland Supply Center through Oakland Harbor, through San Francisco Bay, under the Golden Gate Bridge, and out into open sea.

"Has anyone on board ever taken a ship to sea?" Red asked the crew, as they prepared to leave the pier.

He expected some well-seasoned, experienced sailor to step forward. When none of the men responded, their new skipper got the ship underway himself.

As *Niagara Falls* moved out of Oakland Harbor and into San Francisco Bay, the harbor pilot required by Navy regulations came aboard. Visibility was zero-zero as heavy fog hid the Golden Gate Bridge from view, and foghorns on each end of the gigantic bridge sounded the navigational signals necessary for the ship to circumvent the hundreds of sailboats waiting in the Bay for the annual sailing regatta. Threading his way through the maze of water traffic, Red remembered what Admiral Cousins had said to him when he heard about Red's orders to command *Niagara Falls*.

"We don't send aviators to sea to test their skill, Red. We send aviators to sea to test their luck."

Aviator's luck held, and Red dismissed the harbor pilot when the ship reached open sea. Then, and only then, did some of the ship's experienced officers begin to step forward and offer to handle the ship. In taking the helm himself the day the ship went to sea, Red had proved himself to the crew. For the sixteen months of Red's command, the performance of *Niagara Falls* proved the wisdom of a Navy policy regarding command at sea. The captain of a ship must not only know the ways of the sea; the captain of a ship must also be a leader of men. The captain of USS *Niagara Falls* had paid his dues, and he had won the crew's respect his very first day at sea. Their captain was a leader of men.

It was a little harder for me to prove myself to the wives. I almost had to drown to do it. It was easy with the small group of officers' wives, but I also wanted to bring the enlisted men's wives together, to build the kind of camaraderie and support I knew they needed to cope with their husbands' long deployments. My experience with the POW/MIA wives had taught me the importance of support groups. Not only would the women benefit, but the morale of the crew would be greatly improved. Red had told me how his confidence in me to handle things at home had helped him in his struggle to survive in Hanoi. Even though a seven-

month deployment to the western Pacific wasn't quite the same as
the seven-year separation we had gone through, I knew the principle was the same. The men needed to know everything was under
control at home, if they were to perform the rigorous task of man-
ning a ship at sea. To win over the *Niagara Falls* enlisted wives,
somehow I had to win the confidence of the wife of one of the senior chief petty officers. It was obvious that she was the one the
other wives looked up to, and I could sense that she didn't like me
very much.

Red asked me to meet him in Hong Kong about halfway
through the seven months to make the long separation easier. My
first day in Hong Kong included a trip out into the harbor to meet
Red on the ship for an important ceremony with some of the local
dignitaries. *Niagara Falls* was at anchor several miles out in unusually choppy waters, and the boat crew failed to lash the captain's
gig securely to the Jacob's ladder extending down the side of the
ship. When I stepped from the gig onto the lowest rung of the ladder, the gig moved out and my foot hit open air instead of the ladder. Down I went into Hong Kong Harbor, in my brand new pink
linen suit and spiffy hairdo, taking my expensive new leather
shoulder bag, my passport, and all my travelers' checks with me.

Red was standing at the top of the ladder, all decked out in his
dress white uniform, ready to greet the dignitaries and the television crew expected momentarily. He leaped down the ladder to
help the crew pull me out of the water before the gig lurched back
and crushed me against the hull of the ship. In rescuing me, he cut
a big gash on his forehead and blood began dripping down on his
white uniform, which was also now smudged with black grease.

I was completely oblivious to any danger. I was just mortified,
and in a big hurry to get out of sight before anyone saw me. So I
jumped back into the gig for the trip back to shore, where I got
into a taxi, dripping wet, and sloshed through the elegant plush-
carpeted lobby of our hotel to the elevators. I was determined to
get back to the ship as soon as I possibly could. Knowing Red
would be worried about me, I knew I had to show up at the luncheon to be held in the captain's cabin after the ceremony. I took the
fastest shower of my life, hoping my newly short hair would be dry
by the time I got back aboard. I missed the entire ceremony, but

made it just in time for lunch. The boat crew looked at me sheepishly when I got back into the gig, and they were extremely careful to get me aboard safely this time. And the word went back to Alameda immediately, to the wives of the whole crew:

"The captain's wife fell into Hong Kong Harbor."

And the CPO's wife I had been trying to impress said to the other wives, "My husband said the captain's wife has really got *guts*; she fell into the harbor, but she was back on the ship within the hour."

From that day on, she was my friend.

However, as important as it was to win over the CPO's wife, I would have liked it better if I could have done it another way. Before long, it seemed that everyone in the Navy knew about my escapade in Hong Kong Harbor. When the week in Hong Kong ended, I flew to Manila to meet Red when *Niagara Falls* reached the Philippines. We had reservations in the Visiting Officers' Quarters (VOQ) at NAS Cubi Point, where Red's POW friend Howie Rutledge was commanding officer. Red met my flight and we drove from Manila through the lush tropical countryside to Cubi Point and checked into the VOQ. There was a message at the desk from Captain Rutledge.

"I regret to inform you that the Navy has placed you and your wife 'on report' for unauthorized swimming in Hong Kong Harbor."

My dip into Hong Kong Harbor is going to be a Navy legend, I thought. *I'll never be able to live down that adventure!*

Niagara Falls headed back to California in December, and Red asked Mike and Dave to meet him in Pearl Harbor and come home with him on the ship. The two weeks at sea with his dad gave Mike the little extra push he needed to make the decision to try for admission to the Naval Academy. When he got back to Alameda, he rapidly completed his half-finished application to Annapolis, and told me, "I really admire what my dad does. And I know I need the discipline I will get at the Academy."

"You'll have to cut your hair, Mike," I said.

Mike grinned.

"I hope you didn't think I was going to wear my hair like this forever."

He had survived. He had survived the long separation from his father. He had survived the experience of being uprooted in his last year of high school. And he had survived the sixties in America.

The reward for leadership and outstanding performance as captain of USS *Niagara Falls* was command of an aircraft carrier, every naval aviator's dream. We left California in January of 1977 and drove across the country to Pensacola, Florida, where Red would assume command of USS *Lexington,* the training carrier used by the Navy to allow student pilots to practice making carrier landings at sea.

Another move, less than two years after we'd left Virginia Beach. Now it was Dave's turn to balk. A junior in high school, he had also become an avid surfer, relishing the gigantic waves on the West Coast.

"There're no waves in Pensacola!" he groaned.

"Look on the bright side, Dave," I said. "*Lexington* doesn't stay at sea for months at a time, just two- or three-week training deployments in the Gulf of Mexico."

"The *flat* Gulf of Mexico," he grumbled, his scowl deepening.

"Mike will be around part of the time in Pensacola," I added.

The scowl lifted a little. He had really missed his brother since Mike had graduated and gone on to the Naval Academy. Mike was halfway through his plebe year at Annapolis when Red's book about his experience as a POW, *Before Honor** (published while he had command of *Niagara Falls*), showed up on the shelves of the Mid Store at the Academy. Now a spit-and-polish midshipman, Mike was terribly embarrassed by the pictures in the book of himself with long hair. He gave me a hard time for not making him cut it while he was in high school.

"I take a lot of razzing from the guys about my hair in those pictures," he said when he came home to California for Christmas break in 1976.

"You deserve every word of it," I teased him.

He would spend part of the summer in Pensacola on a mid cruise, so Red's orders to Pensacola meant we could have Mike

---

*Later published in paperback under the title *Scars and Stripes.*

and some of the other mids over for dinner and conversation occasionally.

Leslie wasn't too happy about having to leave her friends. She also wasn't looking forward to living in Navy quarters again. Neither was I, but I was excited for Red. I knew this was the pinnacle of his Navy career. I also was relieved that he would be home with us most nights.

Pensacola was quite an adventure for all of us. The townspeople were proud of *Lexington*, and they treated Red and me like royalty—the king and queen of *Lexington*, *their* ship. Most of *Lexington*'s crew were aviators and we were glad to be back where we belonged, in the naval aviation community. The young student pilots were eager to learn and they looked up to Red as some kind of god, gazing at his rows of medals in awe and begging to hear all about his experiences as a POW. The officers' wives were a close-knit group and the enlisted wives were well-organized and active. Dave and Leslie loved the long stretches of beautiful white sandy beach, the wide variety of water sports, and Dave found that winter storms blowing in from the Gulf would occasionally produce surfing waves that were almost as good as those on the West Coast. I knew that neither of them would want to leave Pensacola, either, when Red's short eighteen-month tour ended.

And I finally did get to see New Orleans.

One morning a few months after Red assumed command of "Lady Lex," he received a call from the commander of Naval Air Atlantic Fleet, Admiral Gus Kinnear.

"How'd you like to take *Lexington* eighty-nine miles up the Mississippi River to New Orleans? Admiral Pierre Charbonnet wants to have his retirement ceremony on a carrier, and he wants to have it in New Orleans.

"I think sending Lady Lex would be great PR for the Navy, and it would sure be good liberty for your crew. You'd be in port for the Muhammad Ali/Leon Spinks fight."

"Are you sure there's enough deep water to get up there from the Gulf?" Red asked. "Sure, we'll give it a go, if there's enough draft."

There was sufficient deep water in the eighty-nine winding miles that made up the Mississippi from the Gulf of Mexico to the city of New Orleans, but it wasn't always easy to locate. And not only did the crew have to keep close tabs on the bottom of the river, they also had to watch for perils overhead. As *Lexington* reached New Orleans and headed for Poydras Pier in the heart of the city, a huge power line that bowed out over the river loomed directly in the path of the gigantic carrier's unhinged mast. The mast extended one hundred and ninety-one feet into the air, so the ship had to veer way over toward the right bank, almost leaving the entrance channel. A close call.

Well, Admiral Cousins, Red chuckled to himself, you said they don't send aviators to sea to test their skill. Looks like they don't send aviators *up the river* to test their skill, either. Here I am, up the Mississippi River, testing my aviator's luck again.

I drove from Pensacola and met Red in the city of my dreams, New Orleans. We saw the city in grand style. The New Orleans Hilton, only a few feet from *Lexington*'s berth, gave us a complimentary four-night stay in the lavish Presidential Suite on the top floor. We sat on the elegant balcony and gazed down at the crew, who looked like ants going about their tasks on the flight deck.

Muhammad Ali wanted a tour of *Lexington*, and Red made certain he was "piped aboard," just like any other distinguished visitor. He wanted the crew to know Ali had arrived so they could hustle up to the flight deck to meet the champ and get his autograph. But most of the men on *Lexington* were appalled that such a military honor was bestowed on a man they considered a draft dodger.

Red, too, decided he had made a mistake treating him like a dignitary when Ali came to his cabin for a visit and asked his first question.

"Do you fly airplanes off this boat?"

His second question wasn't much better.

"How much did this boat cost?" he wanted to know.

Red said his conversation with the heavyweight champion of the world went downhill from there.

Both Red and I knew that his command of a 2,500-man ship would be a big challenge. What we didn't anticipate was the tough job Red would have keeping the thirty-five-year-old carrier seaworthy.

"This ancient ship is a disaster waiting to happen," he exclaimed to me one afternoon when he returned, exhausted, from a two-week training exercise in the Gulf.

Much-needed spare parts were nonexistent. The ship's systems were so outdated that suitable parts were no longer manufactured for them. The maintenance crews on at least one occasion obtained an obsolete part, a condensate pump, from the old USS *Alabama*, now a floating museum in neighboring Mobile Bay. At other times, the crew made their own spare parts and worked around the clock in a herculean effort to keep the systems in relatively safe condition.

"Sometimes my men hold *Lexington* together with nothing more than baling wire and willpower," Red commented late one night, after a grueling day of preparations aboard ship to get underway early the next morning.

"It's a crime. It's a crime to ask those young, inexperienced student pilots to land on that creaking old crate. The nation owes them something better."

But the crew did hold the ship together, and *Lexington* achieved 20,000 carrier landings without a major accident during Red's eighteen-month command. He credited the determination of the 2,500 men of the crew with the aged ship's excellent performance.

"Their average age is only nineteen and one-half years," he said. "The performance of *Lexington* is a tribute to the young people of this country."

I knew the dedication of the young men of *Lexington*, and the outstanding performance of their ship, was also a tribute to the leadership of their captain. As Red and I said goodbye to the crew and their families in November 1978, a twenty-six-year-old first class petty officer said to me, "I'd follow that man to hell and back."

14

On Capitol Hill

B y the time Red left *Lexington*, his anger about national defense priorities was at the boiling point.

"Sailors should not have to hold their ships together with baling wire," he said.

"I rotted away in a communist cell because President Johnson stopped the bombing of North Vietnam to try to win the White House for Hubert Humphrey. For three years those bombers didn't come. For three years our negotiators in Paris argued with the communists about whether to negotiate at a round table or a square table. Now President Carter is dismantling our national defense! They're cutting corners on every defense system we have. We can't even buy a condensate pump for the ship that trains our Navy pilots.

"Seems to me that somebody's priorities are wrong here. It's the pork barrel items in the defense budget that come first. Basics like safe training ships for young aviators get left out. I just don't understand that. Maybe some of the parlor-room patriots on Capitol Hill can explain it to me when I get there," he fumed.

"Cool it, Red," I cautioned. "Don't forget you're a Navy man. President Carter is your commander in chief. Keep your opinions to yourself."

We were headed for Washington, where Red would serve as the Navy's liaison to the U.S. House of Representatives. It was going to be hard for him to stay out of the political debate on Capitol Hill, feeling as strongly as he did about defense policy.

Leslie did not want to leave Pensacola.

"Why do we always have to move during high school?" she complained.

"Your dad will be home nights," I told her. "Mike will be able to come home on weekends and bring some of the other midshipmen with him. Dave's in North Carolina, so we can get our family together more often."

That cheered her up a little. One of the by-products of the ups and downs of our lives was the deep love between Leslie and her brothers. She had borne the full brunt of her father's captivity. Too young to understand war, she had been deeply affected by Red's absence while she was growing up. He had been a stranger to her when he came home. She had held her tears inside and made a valiant effort to learn to love him. But the gap was too wide. Now, in her turbulent teen years, she still sought advice and encouragement primarily from Mike and Dave. The boys were very protective of their little sister and, as busy as they were with their own college activities, they always had time for one of her many long-distance calls to "talk things over."

None of the children had a hometown. We had uprooted them three times since Red came home and, as each one went away to college, "home" was a different place. But they were proud of their dad. And they were beginning to share his sense of mission—and his politics.

Dave was a freshman political science major at the University of North Carolina at Chapel Hill. He spent his summer vacations on Capitol Hill with Red, as an intern in the offices of conservative congressmen. Since Red couldn't say what he thought at work, he used Dave as his sounding board.

"Dave, if we lose our freedom, nothing else matters," he said late one night during one of their marathon political discussions.

"Well, we're going to. Lose our freedom, I mean," David commented.

"Why is that?"

"If you could be a fly on the wall in some of my classes, you'd know why," Dave answered. "The professors don't believe there's any threat out there and the students just swallow everything they hear—hook, line, and sinker. You should see the expressions on their faces. On the students' faces, I mean. They're like dry sponges. They believe whatever the professor says. They don't think; they don't ask questions. They just soak everything up.

"In fact, I should tell you, I'm probably going to get kicked out of school. I'm one of two kids who ask any questions. The professors don't like it one bit. They get flustered. It's like *they* don't think either. They're just quoting something they've read or something someone has told them. They can't defend what they think. They don't know why they think it. That's why they don't want us to question them."

"What's the answer to that, Dave?" Red asked him.

"I don't know. The students just need to hear the other side, probably. They believe anything they hear. I wish you could come down and speak to some of my classes. Although they probably wouldn't let you on campus."

"What could I say?" Red asked.

"Just tell them how it feels to lose your freedom, Dad."

In his office in the basement of the Rayburn House Office Building, Red was getting an education on national defense policymaking. He considered President Jimmy Carter's dismantling of some of America's most strategic defense capabilities to be naive and dangerous. Still, Jimmy Carter was his commander in chief, and Red's mouth was sealed. He was a military man. His was "not to reason why, but to do...and sometimes die."

And it wasn't just President Carter. Everywhere he looked, Red saw a defeatist attitude, in the White House, in the halls of Congress, even within the military itself.

The attitude said, "If you can't beat 'em, join 'em." Red knew his country deserved better, and that it would have to have better, if freedom were to survive.

Even worse than the defeatism was the complacency, the apathy, even on the part of those who sat in positions of national leadership. One of his duties as Navy Liaison was to accompany members of the House of Representatives on trips to other countries. Sometimes the trips were authentic fact-finding missions. Other times, House members were representing the United States at international conferences. Sometimes, the trips were just plea-sure "junkets."

He had been in the Navy Liaison post for several months when he was asked to arrange the transportation and then accom-pany a congressional delegation to Caracas, Venezuela, where the congressmen would represent the United States at a meeting of the Inter-Parliamentary Union.

The first day of the meeting, Red found himself sitting at the U.S. delegation's table all alone. The congressmen had gone shop-ping or to play tennis or to the movies, and left a Navy captain to represent our nation. Representatives of other nations, even the small Third World countries, were high-ranking, polished diplo-mats. When Red came home, he said, "For the first time in my life, I was ashamed to be an American."

Embedded deep in my consciousness were principles planted there by the people of my childhood.

When I was older, I heard a minister say, "Love is not just a feeling; love is a commitment."

Red promised to love me, cherish me, and protect me. He should have added, "And I promise you'll never be bored."

I was so proud of Red when the day came for me to pin his gold Navy wings on his chest.

Mike, eight; David, seven; and Leslie, four, when their dad left for Vietnam in October 1966.

We received this picture from Red of him dressed in combat flying gear just before he was shot down over North Vietnam on May 19, 1967.

Dearest Dorothy, Michael, David, Leslie my health is good in all respects - no permanent injuries you are my inspiration. Children, work, study, play hard, help each other and mommy be strong for our reunion. Invest savings in mutual fund and stock. Your decisions are mine. Dorothy, I love you deeply. Hugs

NGÀY VIẾT (Dated) *15 December 1969*

GHI CHÚ (N B.):

1. Phải viết rõ và chỉ được viết trên những dòng kẻ sẵn (*Write legibly and only on the lines*).

2. Trong thư chỉ được nói về tình hình sức khỏe và tình hình gia đình (*Write only about health and family*).

3. Gia đình gửi đến cũng phải theo đúng mẫu, khuôn khổ và quy định này (*Letters from families should also conform to this proforma*).

Finally, the first letter from Red, dated Dec. 15, 1969, which we received in March 1970.

Every Christmas while Red was a POW we sent him a family picture. This one taken December 21, 1971, was one of the few the Vietnamese allowed him to have.

Mine was a lonely vigil...under the tall stately pine trees at our new home in Virginia Beach.

David at the "Flame of Hope," built in Virginia Beach to remind the public of the missing men in Vietnam.

Volunteer Ann Westerman (right) with Janie Tschudy and me at our POW/MIA headquarters working to get our message out.

The "Phil Donahue Show" was still a regional show at the time, but it was still a big break when Ruth Anne Perisho, Janie Tschudy, and I appeared on the Dec. 17, 1969, show. Phil is holding Red's picture for the camera.

"My husband, Eugene, is a Lieutenant-Commander in the Navy. He's been a prisoner in Vietnam for 4 years. They're bargaining to get the prisoners released. But what I want to know... is he still alive? Is he well? I can't find out. Hanoi won't tell our government. Hanoi won't tell me."

There need be no "bargaining table" when the plea is for humane treatment of prisoners of war.

THE prisoner-of-war issue is complex and confusing. It is loaded with political overtones and emotional tension.

But one side of the prisoner-of-war issue is simple. That's the part which deals with the <u>condition</u> of prisoners.

Who are they? Where are they? How are they?

Those are the questions the families of American prisoners want answered. Those are the questions the conscience of the world wants answered...now.

Of course, they want the war to end and the prisoners of war to be released as soon as possible.

But meanwhile there is no need for Hanoi and its allies to delay even a day in answering this plea:

Admit official neutral observers into the prison camps in North Vietnam, South Vietnam, Cambodia and Laos, where Americans are being held in secret captivity.

Assure the world, through these neutral observers, that American prisoners are being decently and humanely treated, according to the standards of civilized nations.

Hanoi can do this without bargaining, even without consultation.

By opening the prisons now to official neutral observers, Hanoi would earn the gratitude of millions of Americans and find new stature in the eyes of the world.

We ask and pray they will.

SUPPORT OUR PLEA TO HANOI AND ITS ALLIES:

Clear away the doubts —
Open your prison camps to neutral observers...
now!

We ask no more than we give. All American and South Vietnamese prison camps are inspected regularly by official neutral observers — The International Committee of the Red Cross.

✚ American Red Cross

Advertising contributed for the public good ⓐ

National League of Families of American Prisoners and Missing in Southeast Asia.
1608 "K" Street, N.W. Washington, D.C. 20006

This ad ran in newspapers and magazines across the nation in 1969 and 1970.

It's January 1973, and we just learned Red will be coming home "within the next sixty days."

The Vietnamese turned Red over to U.S. custody on March 4, 1973, at Gia Lam Airport, Hanoi.

When his plane was diverted because of the weather, we were to be whisked off immediately to the Portsmouth Naval Hospital while the crowd was informed that the men they had waited to see wouldn't be landing after all. But I insisted that the wives thank the crowd ourselves, and the Navy brass accompanied us out into the rain.

Thousands of people from Tidewater, Virginia, stood in the rain to welcome Red and three other POWs from Tidewater home.

After six long years, we were finally together again.

Red literally swept Leslie off her feet.

A huge hand-lettered banner stretched from one side of our street to the other.

Friends and neighbors in Virgina Beach welcome their hero home.

Mike and his dad at the U.S. Naval Academy, Parents' Weekend, "Plebe Summer" 1976.

David, Leslie, and I went aboard USS *Niagara Falls* to attend the ceremony for Red to assume command of his first ship.

We tried to provide support and encouragement for the families of the men under Red's command. Mike, home on leave, joined Red and me at a Christmas party for the crew of USS *Lexington*.

In 1975, Red and I visited San Clemente, where Red
gave former President Nixon a copy of his book *Scars
and Stripes*.

Congressman Vander Jagt encouraged Red to run for
Congress and then came down to North Carolina to
campaign for him. The whole family rallied behind Red,
with everyone pitching in to help with his campaign.

As founder and president of the American Defense Institute, Red could continue to speak to and for the young people who had rallied behind him in his unsuccessful bid for Congress.

Red and I listen during a speech made by President Reagan when he came to North Carolina to campaign for Red in 1982. Over the years Red supported most of the president's policies, but on the POW issue he veered sharply away.

In 1986, Leslie, wearing her dad's POW uniform, marched to the White House in chains with sons and daughters of men still missing.

When Mike became executive director of the American Defense Institute, he told Red, "I like what you're doing, Dad, and I want to have a part in it."

My parents, Charles and Alma Howard. "You'll never be happy if you base your life on your feelings," my father taught me.

The entire McDaniel family gathered on Feb. 23, 1990, for Leslie's marriage to Jim Lindsay.

Photo by Ed O'Reilly

15

The Under-Thirty Crowd

Halfway through Red's tour of duty on Capitol Hill, Ronald Reagan was elected president of the United States. Red was elated.

"Today is the happiest day of my life!" he said to his good friend, Congressman Guy Vander Jagt. "And that includes the day I was released from prison. That day was a release for me. Today is a release for America."

Congressman Vander Jagt quoted Red in his speeches and in his book, *A Country Worth Saving*, ending Red's discreet silence concerning political affairs.

Seated in the front row at President Reagan's inauguration in January 1981, we listened to the new president promise to rebuild America's defense capability.

Later, at one of the inaugural balls, Red told the president how his election had restored Red's hope for America's future.

"Six years in a communist prison gives a man time to reflect on where his country is headed. Since I came home, I have watched my country gamble with our freedom.

"Congratulations, Mr. President. And thank you for what you are going to do for our country."

Congressman Vander Jagt's task as chairman of the National Republican Congressional Committee was to recruit Republican candidates to run for Congress. I knew he was working on Red.

So I wasn't surprised when Red walked in the door one night in February 1981, and announced he wanted to retire from the Navy.

"We're going home to North Carolina and I'm going to run for Congress. I want to help Ronald Reagan turn this great country around," he said excitedly.

I agreed that it was time for Red to leave the Navy. He needed to be where he could say what he thought, and perhaps have a small part in making the decisions that affected our freedom.

But run for Congress?

We knew next to nothing about political campaigns. Democrats outnumbered Republicans in eastern North Carolina by a huge margin. Voters there were interested in local issues: the tobacco subsidy, welfare, interstate highways, and the other bread-and-butter issues that touched their daily lives. Red cared about national defense, about the threats to our country's freedom, about protecting that freedom. We had been away from home for twenty-seven years. Perhaps we should move back to North Carolina, reestablish ourselves with the people there, feel out the political climate, and then run for Congress in a few years.

"No, we have to seize the moment," Red said. "The country's turning around *now!* I want to do my part."

"But, Red, isn't there something you can do here in Washington, without running for Congress?"

"Sure, I could go to work for one of the defense contractors. I know Capitol Hill. I could make some money. Maybe I should do that. You deserve it," he said, with a downcast look.

The truth was I didn't want to leave Washington. I didn't want to give up my job. After twenty-seven years of being wife and mother—Navy wife, POW wife—I had decided to do something for me. My teaching career had been sporadic, and I had given it up altogether after Red was shot down, except to substitute teach occasionally. After Leslie graduated from high school and went off to college, I had gotten a job in a congressional office as a press secretary. The writing and press experience I had gained from working with the POW/MIA publicity campaigns was good preparation for working on Capitol Hill. During the desperate days of Red's captivity, I had given no thought to any long-term benefit to me from the effort to keep Red in the public eye. It had been a life-or-death struggle born of my anxiety about him. Now, however, I realized how much I had learned during those hard years, and how valuable—and marketable—my knowledge really was.

In the years following Red's return, I had settled back into my wife-and-mother cocoon, gratefully moving aside for Red to take his place as head of the family, reaching out only to the wives of the men under Red's command. Now I was using the press skills I had learned. I loved my job, and I didn't want to give it up, even for my country.

In the congressional office where I handled the press activities, I had seen enough of the rough-and-tumble of politics to know that Red would, for the first time in his life, have his integrity questioned. How anyone would be able to damage his reputation, I couldn't imagine. But I knew they would try, and I was afraid for him.

"But how can we win?" I asked him.

"We have to try," he answered.

The one big advantage I saw in our moving back to North Carolina was that we would finally have a real home, a permanent place.

We can settle down. I can find a wall for my favorite painting, and it can stay there. Also, we would be near Red's mother and my parents, who were all getting older. We could be with them in their later years. We would be where our roots were, after twenty-seven years of wandering in service to our country.

We found the perfect house. I loved every inch of it. *Here we are, back where we belong,* I said to myself as the moving van pulled out of the driveway. *Red's retired now. After all those hard years, why don't we just settle in and enjoy ourselves? Why run for anything? We've done enough.* The golf course was an easy walk from our house. Childhood friends lived close by. The small-town pace of life appealed to me, although I knew it would take some getting used to.

We moved in just before Christmas. Dave arrived a few days later.

"I'm home, Dad," he announced. "I've dropped out of college to help you in your campaign. I don't know much about campaigning, but I believe in the candidate. So put me to work."

"I don't expect you to do that, Dave," Red answered. "You've got other things to do. And I'm not sure you should drop out of college in the middle of your junior year."

"Look, all my life I've needed you. Now you need me, and here I am," Dave grinned.

Leslie was halfway through her freshman year at East Carolina University. She walked in the front door with all her belongings as soon as the semester ended in December.

"I'm not going back until after the campaign. I want to help you win, Dad. They need you in Congress," she said with finality.

Red was dumbfounded. I think it was the first time he realized just how much he meant to his children.

So much for retirement. The campaign's already started.

All four of us hit the campaign trail early in February. Dave raised the money. Leslie manned the computer in Red's campaign headquarters. Red and I crisscrossed the district in rural North Carolina, shaking hands at country stores and crossroads, speaking to small Republican gatherings and trying to talk to as many Democrats as possible, one-on-one. When I wasn't making campaign appearances, I was working on Red's speeches and press releases. Once again, the experience I had gained during the feverish POW/MIA publicity campaigns was standing us in good stead, as was the knowledge gained from my work as a Capitol Hill press secretary. But my job on Capitol Hill had made me too aware of the issues for my own good. The campaign consultants wanted me to stick to ladies' coffees, sharing recipes and homemaking tips. I wanted to talk about more substantive things. But to keep peace in the campaign, I tried to follow their instructions. I understood now why some of the "candidate schools" sponsored by the political parties had seminars with such titles as "How to Deal with the Candidate's Spouse."

By April everything was ready for Red's formal announcement. We persuaded as many supporters as possible to gather in three different parts of the district. Red and I flew in a small plane to the three locations on the same day for him to make his announcement speech. To heavy press coverage and the cheers of his already fiercely loyal supporters, Red stood under "McDaniel for Congress" banners and signs to tell the people of the Third District how much he loved his country:

> When I returned home after six years in a communist prison, I saw an America in trouble. Our national defense was crumbling.

We had lost the respect of the world community. Big government was out of control. Well-meaning measures that we had taken to make life easier had grown into monsters that threatened to devour us. The moral fiber of our nation was disintegrating. A sense of helplessness and frustration was sapping our national spirit.

He talked about the career experiences that had given him insight into national policymaking, including his tour on Capitol Hill, which had also taught him "how to get things done in that bureaucratic no-man's land on the Potomac." He expressed his confidence in the Reagan administration's ability to change the things that needed to be changed. Then he asked his audience if the nation should hold a "steady course" and finish what Reagan started in 1980, or "go back to the mistaken policies of the past?"

Because I believe the answer to that question is crucial to our survival as a free nation, I offer myself as candidate for the United States Congress from the Third District. It is with a deep sense of commitment and humility that I declare my candidacy; commitment, to the goals of a better North Carolina and United States; humility, in the acknowledgment that only by the blessings of God and liberty are these goals possible.

Seated behind him on the podium in Elizabethtown, the last stop of the day, I looked into the sea of faces. *If there's any way to make it happen, these people will make it happen,* I thought. *He's exciting to them. He gives them hope that things can be better. He gives them hope that it is possible to have a representative from this rural district who will make them proud; who will work, not just for the everyday concerns of the people here, but for the greater good of the nation.*

I had never heard Red make a more impassioned speech. He went into some detail about local concerns and then he once again appealed to their patriotism and idealism.

...America's best years are yet to come...With your help, with your support, we will win in November and together we will make America stronger and better tomorrow than she is today.

The applause was deafening. The crowd cheered, and clamored to shake his hand. *Who knows, maybe we can beat the odds and pull this off. One thing's for sure, they'll never have a better candidate. But then I'm a little biased,* I thought ruefully.

Several of Red's friends in Congress came down to North Carolina to campaign for him, including Congressman Vander Jagt, who had talked him into running in the first place. Most of them were astounded at the size of the task of running for a national office in such a rural area, the difficulty of getting a crowd of any size together, and the number of appearances a candidate had to make to reach the voters.

Just before election day, President Reagan made a campaign appearance with Red and called him a "true American hero":

> A POW in North Vietnam, he was condemned to a living hell of torture for a period of a long six years. But the communists hadn't reckoned on this man's courage. They didn't realize you can't destroy the spirit of a true American hero. You can't trample on his faith; you can't kill his feelings of hope and love...In his book *Scars and Stripes*, Red McDaniel wrote that the greatest moment of his life was seeing his wife Dorothy waiting with open arms, a reunion he'd dreamed about every night for those six years. And when he threw his arms around his family, he said it was worth it all for this moment.

Looking out at the exuberant crowd, I heard the president tell the people of the Third District that courageous men like Red were sorely needed in Washington. *Surely they can see, surely they can see that this man who's offering himself to represent them will be head and shoulders above the others. There won't be a man in Washington who loves our country more than Red does!*

It was Bill Lacy who first noticed how many of the volunteers in Red's campaign were in their teens and twenties. Bill was a field director for the National Republican Congressional Committee. It was his job to help direct Red's campaign.

"Red, you've attracted hundreds of young people. They're newcomers. They don't know politics. They've never been involved before. But here they are, working for you."

"Well, let's hope a lot of them vote. We're going to need them," Red replied.

Dave had raised over $500,000—a phenomenal sum in that rural part of the state. Red was up at dawn every day, going back and forth across the district. Leslie was doing the job of three people at campaign headquarters. I was speaking five and six times a week.

But it was obvious we weren't going to win. Red was running against an entrenched incumbent who was just completing his third term in office. Very few of the Democrats we talked to could bring themselves to vote for a Republican candidate. They told Red how much they admired him, and many of them said they knew he would be a more effective representative than anyone they'd ever elected, but that he was just in the wrong political party. All my life I had voted for the *person*, not the party, and I just could not understand where these people, some of them our very good friends, were coming from. But political party was the important thing, and no matter what we did, the numbers just weren't there.

Why are we doing this to ourselves? I knew we weren't going to win, and my heart was breaking for Red. He had given up his Navy career and he had tried so hard. He wouldn't handle losing very well. *God, what is your purpose in all of this? We don't need this, not at this point in our lives.*

The "victory party" on election night brought hundreds of young people to the Howard Johnson's restaurant in Dunn, North Carolina. They came to celebrate the victory of their hero and candidate, Red McDaniel. In his campaign, they had learned about politics. They had learned about the threat to freedom. They had learned why America needs to be strong.

And they had lost an election. Considering the odds, they had done remarkably well. But they had lost.

I felt worse for the young people and the other volunteers who had worked so hard in the campaign than I did for us. I couldn't shake the feeling that we had somehow let them down, even though we had done our best. I hoped these bright youngsters would not give up on politics. They had so much energy and enthusiasm; they had such great dreams.

America needs them, I thought, *as I gazed into their downcast faces.* The older people had pretty much resigned themselves to losing elections. Year after year they had fought a losing Republican battle against a one-party system, against entrenched incumbents. But the young people, I hoped, would try again.

When the campaign dust had settled, Bill Lacy approached Red.

"Remember the hundreds of youngsters who flocked to your campaign? You owe them something, you know."

Red stared at him.

"I don't follow you," he said.

"I think you have to find a way to use the influence you have with the under-thirty crowd. No matter what you say to them, they believe you," Bill said, leaning forward on his elbows, his brown eyes searching Red's fatigue-lined face.

"That's true. I have to watch what I say to them. I suppose they see me as something of an enigma, a man who should be dead but isn't. They can't figure out just what makes me tick, why I'm so determined to have my say, why I don't just sit back and smell the roses.

"Well, I can't do that. Smell the roses, I mean. Those kids—they're great kids, you know—those kids just don't know what's happening. They're bright-eyed and bushy-tailed, and we've let them down."

Red looked out the window and down the quiet residential street with its manicured lawns and serene, stately houses.

"Those kids think everything's safe and secure. They've grown up on quiet streets like this one, and then gone off to college where they've listened wide-eyed to lectures from professors in ivory towers about the way to have a peaceful world. We just have to trust each other, they're told. They believe America is the aggressor. They have no earthly idea why Communism is a threat to us. They think freedom is permanent, that nothing can happen on streets like this one. They're so *gullible!*"

"Right," Bill said. "And who's going to straighten them out? You are!"

"Me? I just lost an election, remember?"

Bill reached into his jacket pocket and looked at the time on his plane ticket.

"Gotta run, Red. Listen, I want you to think about three things. Number one, you have a fire in your belly to do something about the things that threaten our freedom. Number two, you have a natural following among young people. Number three, you may not know it, but a lot of people care just as much as you do. They just don't know what to do about it.

"Let's put it all together and *do* something."

And he was on his way back to Washington.

16

A New Venture

I had never seen Red look so drained, not even when he had walked down the ramp of the C-141 at Clark Air Force Base in 1973. The ruthless, seven-day-a-week pace of the campaign had almost done him in. His shoulders sagged. His eyes were glazed from lack of sleep. His normally buoyant spirit was gone. He had desperately wanted to win, and even though his campaign had paved the way for future Republican candidates in that Democratic stronghold of North Carolina, he was dejected, feeling that he had let a lot of hard-working people down. He had offered himself to the people of the Third District, *his people,* and he had been turned down.

A cruise to the Caribbean. That's what we need now. We've talked about it for years, but we've never had the time. What we need is to get away, bask in the sun, doze in the deck chairs, and forget politics. We've done our share. Now it's someone else's turn. After Christmas we'll head for the Caribbean and a well-deserved vacation.

Just before Christmas, Dave and Leslie went with us to the airport to meet Mike and his new bride Debbie, home from California for the holidays. Being on active duty with the Navy had precluded Mike from helping out with the campaign, and he was full of questions about why we had lost.

"The numbers just weren't there, son," Red said soberly. "We gave it our best shot. There's nothing you could have done about it if you'd been here. It was what some people would call a 'suicide mission.'"

Later, as we settled in front of the fire in our family room, savoring the warmth of the blaze and the warm bonds of love we shared with our children, we sensed the rest and peace that always seemed to magically descend upon our family at Christmastime. I could see the twinkle slowly returning to Red's eyes as Dave and Leslie regaled Mike and Deb with tales from the campaign, leaving them howling with laughter. Dave told them about the time one of the campaign workers was supposed to send newsletters to all the "*elected* officials" in the district, meaning mayors, city councilmen, and other people in similar positions. The worker misunderstood and sent the newsletters to all the *election* officials, who made up the nucleus of the opposition.

"Here we were sending our battle plans right into the enemy's camp," Dave laughed.

Then Leslie told them about the time the opposition had attacked Red for using his military retirement benefits.

"I'll bet McDaniel even buys his groceries on a military base," a local Democratic leader had claimed.

The McDaniel for Congress campaign, tongue in cheek, had issued a press release stating that "Red McDaniel is making available for the public record the names of the stores where he does his grocery shopping. The McDaniels buy their groceries at the A&P, the Winn-Dixie store, and the Piggly Wiggly grocer."

But when Dave started telling them about election day, when two farmers had chased him away from a polling place with an ax, Mike said he'd had enough.

"Dad, you could've called in the FBI on that one," he said. "That's tampering with a federal election! Not only that, but you could've gotten yourself killed, Dave."

"Anything for the cause!" Leslie laughed.

"Well, I'm glad you kept your sense of humor," Mike added. "I still don't know why you had to put yourself through that, Dad. You've already done your part."

But the campaign had brought us all closer together. It had also paved Red's way to an even greater mission.

In January, as we lay side-by-side on the pearl-white sand, half-dozing in the Caribbean sun after an afternoon of snorkling in the bright blue-green ocean, Red mumbled to me, "Bill's right. I owe them something."

"Um? Who?" I opened one eye.

"The under-thirty crowd," he murmured, squinting in the hot sun, eyes scanning the horizon.

I decided not to ask him any questions. The sun was too warm; the sky was too blue. The leisure of lying here beside him without a care in the world was too enticing. I turned over and closed my eyes, lulled by the gentle rhythmic lapping of the blue-green ripples along the shore.

* * *

The sea and the sun worked their magic, and the bounce was back in Red's step by the time the seven-day cruise ended. I had almost forgotten his comment on the beach about the "under-thirty crowd" until one day in February when he announced he was going to Washington "to talk to Bill Lacy." Four days later he was back.

"We're going to name it the American Defense Foundation," Red told me as he got into the seat beside me, slamming the car door behind him.

I pulled out into the heavy traffic leaving the Raleigh-Durham airport.

"Bill says we should rent a small office, or a corner of one, whatever we can afford, on Capitol Hill. We'll use our old campaign headquarters here for most of the work. I can commute back and forth when I need to be in Washington."

"Wait a minute. Slow down. Just what is it we're going to call the American Defense Foundation?" I braked to a stop behind a yellow school bus and looked over at him.

His blue eyes were shining.

"It's a natural," he said, grinning at me. "It's a way for me—and you—to tell young people what they need to know about freedom. About why they have to learn as much as they can, and get ready *now*, if they want to live in freedom tomorrow!

"I'm going to tell them how it feels to lose your freedom, how it feels to have somebody telling you when to sleep, when to get up, when to eat, *what* to eat; how it feels to lie awake at night listening for the turnkey to take you out for another beating to make you say what they want you to say! I'm going to tell them it *can* happen!"

I took a deep breath. The school bus had turned off the main road, and I eased the blue and white Ford into the traffic lane for the right-hand turn that would take us to the peaceful little college town where we could finally retire and settle down after our many years of wandering and the grueling political race.

Bill Lacy was right, I thought. *He does have a fire in his belly. He had it that day nine years ago on the front steps when he told our neighbors in Virginia Beach what had brought him through the torture, the long nights in solitary confinement, the endless days of tossing his wad of dirty bandages into the musty air of his prison cell.* He was a man who loved freedom—and would do whatever it took to protect it.

We were nearing the sharp curve by the water tower on the outskirts of our little town.

"How does it work, Red? And who's going to pay for it?"

"We'll sell the house in Virginia Beach," he answered. "We'll write to all the people who think like I do, starting with the people who contributed to my campaign. My POW friends will help. I believe there are a lot of people out there who want to get involved with something like this.

"You can answer the phone in the office here. You can also do the newsletters and the press releases. You can use what you learned working on Capitol Hill.

"Also," he said, "a lot of my friends on the Hill will help. I've already asked some of the congressmen to be on my board."

The tires crunched on the gravel driveway.

"Your *board?*"

"We incorporated the American Defense Foundation while I was in Washington," he said. "We're underway!"

I followed him up the walk and watched him unlock the oak-panelled front door. The floodlight illuminated his bent head and shoulders.

He's getting gray, I noticed. Where had the time gone? When would he rest?

And then, suddenly, the thought came to me: *our whole lives have been preparing us for this. Those awful six years while he was gone, his time on Capitol Hill, my time on Capitol Hill, that hectic losing campaign for Congress—our whole lives, God has been preparing us for this!*

17

The American Defense Institute

G reg MacCauley looked up from the carton of books he was packing.

"Red's gone. You just missed him."

I was holding Red's overcoat. The temperature had dropped fourteen degrees since morning and I had raced over to our old campaign headquarters, hoping to catch him before he caught the plane for Washington.

"He left these letters for you to type. I was going to drop them by your house on my way home. He said they need to go out in tomorrow morning's mail."

"Thanks, Greg," I sank into the worn green chair just inside the door of the tiny office. "Why did he decide to go today? He was planning to leave in the morning, and then he called to say he was leaving. Do you know why he changed his mind?" I asked him.

"They're voting on Contra Aid tonight instead of tomorrow," Greg told me. "Red wanted to catch some of the members on their way in before they vote. He thinks he can change a couple of minds."

I picked up the folder of letters.

"I'll be back in a minute," Greg said. "I have to get these books to the post office so they'll go out today. They're for Red's speech at Western Carolina University next week."

And he raced out the door.

Greg was a college sophomore who had worked as a volunteer in Red's campaign, and he was the first to volunteer to work at the American Defense Foundation office. When he wasn't in class, he was answering the phone and taking care of the mail and handling other various and sundry tasks. He told us he wanted to go into politics some day, but right now he wanted a piece of the action in what he called "Red's plan to get young people like me moving in the right direction."

It had been Greg's idea to have Red give the students paperback copies of his book, *Scars and Stripes*, when he spoke on a college campus. From the beginning, the Foundation had mailed copies of the book to contributors and to people we hoped would contribute to our effort to promote a strong defense and teach young people about freedom and patriotism.

One of the first things Red had done as soon as the American Defense Foundation was incorporated was write a letter to his campaign supporters and our personal friends.

Dear Friends,

Happy New Year! Looking back over 1982, we count your friendship as one of our greatest blessings. It was your strong support that made my congressional race in the Third District possible.

Looking ahead in 1983, as we seek direction for the future, we are grateful for the many words of encouragement that have come from you, our friends. In you we have found the courage and the inspiration we need to continue to work for the principles that we share with you.

One thing is clear: our political involvement must be a continuing involvement if we are to have any impact on our government and our national life. We can't just get excited and work hard in an election year. There is too much to be done and too much is at stake. America's future is too precious.

So, for the time being, FRIENDS OF RED McDANIEL will continue to operate as a campaign committee. We're keeping our office open here, accepting as many speaking invitations as possible, and devoting a good deal of time to the formation of a defense education foundation.

THE AMERICAN DEFENSE FOUNDATION will function independently while sharing headquarters with FRIENDS OF RED McDANIEL and will serve as a vehicle to help our people become more aware of the dangers that threaten our nation. We want to focus attention on the need to reaffirm the principles that made America a great nation. We want to talk about the need for a strong national defense. We particularly want to reach our young people—the key to the future.

May God grant you a sense of excitement about the potential for good that the new year will bring.

Red's letter brought a tremendous response from people who believed in him and wanted to help him with his future mission. Many of those who wrote sent contributions to the American Defense Foundation and encouraged him to devote as much time as he could to the education of young Americans.

When Greg got back from mailing the books, he wanted to talk.

"Red tells me you're thinking about moving back to Washington," he said. "If you do, I want to go with you."

"I'm not sure, Greg," I said. "We've talked about it. Red spends one heck of a lot of time going back and forth. We're almost an hour from the airport here. But that tiny office on Capitol Hill isn't going to hold all of us. Anyway, you're still in school. Your parents aren't going to let you drop out and move to Washington, are they?"

"I could take classes there—at American or George Washington," Greg countered.

"Well, we don't know what we're going to do. I hate the thought of pulling up stakes again, although Red does need to be in Washington most of the time," I said and switched on my typewriter.

I knew it was coming. The American Defense Foundation was growing by leaps and bounds. Red had rented one corner of one room in the Heritage Foundation Building in Washington, two blocks from the Hart Senate Office Building. Two rented desks, one telephone, and a typewriter were squeezed into the corner where Janet Prescott Day held forth as our "Washington presence."

Janet was a twenty-six-year-old who had grown up and attended college in the Northeast, where liberalism was the order of the day. For some reason, her ultra-liberal education had had just the opposite of the effect intended. She was a staunch conservative. She instinctively understood Red's dream for the Foundation.

"If you hadn't started it, I would have," she told him over the phone. She had seen Red on television talking about the fledgling defense organization he had started and had called him to ask for a job.

"I want to help you with it," she continued. "The Foundation has the potential of reaching thousands of young people. I would say you have a captive audience because of your POW experience. Everybody is interested in hearing about that, especially youngsters."

It was Janet who envisioned the seminars, fellowships, and internships that formalized Red's effort to reach out to young Americans. She helped him focus his energy on public appearances, especially on college campuses. Having just graduated from college herself, she knew what would appeal to the current student population.

Since most of the programs were educational, the Foundation established a sister organization and called it the American Defense Institute. The Foundation worked to influence defense legislation, and the Institute disseminated defense information to the public, especially to young people. As Red said, "I learned in my campaign that most people over thirty have minds like eight-day-old cement. You can't change them. They're set. It's the young people we have to reach. They're the ones who'll listen."

Once again, we were in unfamiliar territory. None of us knew how to make it all work. And we were all amazed that it did work—and worked very well. People all over the nation responded to our appeals. Congressmen Red had worked with during his tour as Navy/Marine Corps Liaison were eager to lend their names and help Red get the two organizations off the ground. The students who flocked to Red McDaniel when he appeared on their campuses began to compete for the fellowships and internships offered by the Institute. My experience on Capitol Hill once again proved valuable, and I could see how my work on the POW campaigns during the war had prepared me to tackle a whole new agenda.

The task we had given ourselves when we set up our tiny shop for the American Defense Foundation was formidable. We were banking on the power of the grassroots to change things. I, for one, had no doubt that Red could start a national organization. He had the necessary *passion* to do it! And so did Greg and Janet and the other young people who joined the staffs as the two organizations grew.

I had learned that dedication to the effort counted for much more than know-how and experience. So many of the people the POW/MIA wives had enlisted for "Operation We Care" back in Virginia Beach had thought we were beating our heads against a wall, fighting for a lost cause. *But they cared enough to join anyway.* Newspaper editors had not believed their editorials and feature stories would help, but they were moved by our appeal and they ran the articles anyway. In the beginning, they were probably only trying to make us feel better. They were the only ones surprised when those efforts succeeded.

I knew that a few naive, inexperienced POW/MIA wives had been able to start a grassroots movement which had resulted in the adoption of a more humane policy toward POWs by Hanoi—and a commitment from Washington to bring the men home. Red believed that my efforts had affected his life in Hanoi. In fact, he said they had saved him.

"You know, Dorothy, I would not have survived another brutal beating like the one they gave me in May of 1969. But they left me alone after that, for about five months. They still wanted me to write a confession of my 'war crimes.' But since I'd lost the use of my hands as a result of the May beatings, they didn't pressure me for it until I could hold a pencil again.

"In October of 1969, the guards took me back to the torture room and I remember thinking, 'I'll never make it this time.' I was still weak from the last beating, back in May. But when I arrived, the camp commander was there and he was almost civil to me, which he'd never been before. He ordered me to write a confession and I refused.

" 'We can force you to write it,' he reminded me.

" 'I know you can. Well, you'll have to force me,' I responded shakily.

"Then the camp commander said something that was completely out of character.

" 'Don't make us force you,' he said. 'When we force you, it makes us look bad in the eyes of the world.' And he ordered the guards to take me back to my cell.

"I was astounded. I just couldn't figure out for the life of me why he'd said what he'd said. I told the other two guys in my cell about it and one of them said, 'Somebody must be talking about us somewhere. Otherwise, why would he say something about looking bad in the eyes of the world?'"

"Red," I said excitedly, "that was the theme of the JayCees' campaign in 1969, 'The world is watching.' They used a big eye in their logo! I knew it! I knew the Hanoi government would hear that!"

There were so many things I hadn't told him about the years he was gone. And I still didn't know everything that had happened to him during those six years. He had held nothing back, and neither had I. The intimacy that we had shared since early in our marriage had grown deeper in the years since his return. There was never a need to mince words or hold back.

But six years was a long time. I wondered if we would ever catch up. We had moved the old Navy footlocker with my POW/MIA files from Virginia Beach to California to Pensacola to Alexandria to North Carolina, storing it in every attic, but we had never opened it. There just hadn't been time, and neither one of us was very interested in looking back.

I had told Red a lot about our effort to move the Hanoi government, but very little about the need I had felt to make him important to the politicians in Washington. That was not what he wanted to hear.

"You have to have blind faith in your government to survive in a POW camp, Dorothy," he said. "I don't expect you to understand that."

But I did understand it. President Nixon was his hero. Even when most Americans were down on Nixon for the failings exposed by Watergate, Red was a Nixon loyalist.

"He brought me home, Dorothy," he would say whenever anyone began to criticize President Nixon.

He had no choice. We made you so important to the American people that the politicians had to bring you home, I wanted to say. But I didn't say it. He didn't want to hear it. And I had begun to believe Red might be right. His faith in the administration in power when he came home was so convincing that I hoped he *was* right. It didn't seem important now, anyway.

The important thing was to get on with this exciting new venture, the American Defense Institute. It was a way for Red to work with President Reagan to rebuild a strong defense—and to prepare young Americans to appreciate and preserve freedom.

But to do it effectively, Red needed to be in Washington all the time. So in 1984, we moved back to our home in Alexandria, near beautiful Mount Vernon. Greg came, too, his parents having been assured by Red that he would "make sure Greg takes classes in Washington."

We rented new space, our own office! It was still too small for the expanding staff, and we had to severely limit the number of college interns we accepted each semester, sometimes rotating them between our office, the Library of Congress, and congressional offices.

But we could see the impact we were having on the minds and hearts of the energetic young people we met. I had never seen Red happier.

"All my life has been preparing me to do this," he said to me the day we said goodbye to the first group of students to complete their semester-long internships at ADI.

"They changed their minds about things while they were here. And, you know, Dorothy, I have to be careful what I tell them. They do believe anything I say!'

"Well, they're open to suggestion," I countered. "But they're sharp. Give them all the facts. They'll come to the right conclusions."

18

The Right Thing to Do

Most of the issue positions held by the American Defense Foundation and the American Defense Institute were right on target with Ronald Reagan's policies. We supported the president's defense budget, his request for a 600-ship Navy, aid to freedom fighters in Central America, Angola and Afghanistan, and other administration policy positions.

But on one issue Red McDaniel veered sharply from the party line. And he would pay dearly for that difference. He was unwilling to play on a team that ignored evidence that some of his fellow POWs did not come home when he did and were, in fact, still locked up in prison cells in Southeast Asia.

Red had started asking questions about the missing men in 1981, while he was representing the Navy on Capitol Hill. He told me about the "red flags" that had gone up as he accompanied members of Congress to the Pentagon for the POW/MIA briefings. He was haunted by the photograph of what looked like a POW camp in Laos that he had seen in one of the briefings. The satellite camera had captured on film small figures, thought to be Asians, hunkered down in the outer compound of the camp. An inner compound held taller figures, obviously non-Asians. Americans? If not, then who were they? Guard towers were visible at the four corners of the compound, so it was almost certainly a prison. But what had really captured Red's attention was a small cultivated area which looked like some kind of vegetable garden. Stamped out in the vegetable rows, clearly visible from the air, was unmistakably the number 52. Yank ingenuity, he said to himself. An American B-52 crew? It had to be somebody's desperate attempt to get the attention of an overhead flight or orbiting satellite.

He wondered how many other photographs of POW camps were in the Pentagon files, how many live sighting reports from refugees. He suspected there was quite a bit of highly-classified evidence that Americans were still in captivity all over Southeast Asia. However, his faith in Ronald Reagan was absolute. He told himself that Reagan would act on this very persuasive information, and probably even now had some secret negotiations working or rescue missions underway to bring the men home.

My country would *never* abandon a fighting man, he reminded himself.

But the nagging questions wouldn't go away. No action had been taken even as late as 1985. Horror stories about hidden evidence began to filter into his office from a network of Vietnam veterans and POW activists. POW/MIA families told him mind-boggling tales of accidentally discovering intelligence information about their sons and husbands still alive in captivity, and what appeared to be attempts by U.S. officials to explain the evidence away.

At first, Red tried to reassure the family members who approached him.

"Ronald Reagan is the first president since the end of the war who has tried to do anything to find out about any remaining POWs and bring them home," he told the son of a pilot who had bailed out of an Air Force fighter/bomber over Laos in 1971. "He won't let you down. You just have to have faith in the man. He's really committed to this issue."

"It's all a bunch of rhetoric, Captain McDaniel," the young man replied bitterly. "Oh, I believe Reagan cares about the men, or did at first, when he thought there were some still alive. But I believe the people who control the issue don't show the president all the evidence. I don't know why, but I think they want him to believe they're all dead. But they don't want to tell the families that. They know there will be an uproar if they do. The rhetoric is designed to keep us in line.

"There's a reporter I want you to talk to, Red. He's got it all figured out. He's been digging in the National Archives. Most of the stuff about POWs is still classified, but he found some memos from the Nixon White House in the Archives that explain how they kept the families in line during the war. They're still doing it."

"Dorothy will be interested in seeing those," Red responded. "She's always believed there was an orchestrated bureaucratic effort to placate the POW wives. Bring him to see me."

When the POW son and the reporter brought the White House memoranda to his office, Red introduced me to them and handed me the papers. A memo dated April 26, 1971, from White House Chief of Staff H.R. Haldeman to General Hughes, the aide who handled the POW/MIA wives during the war, said, in part:

With the demonstrations gaining ground after the veterans' effort last week, we've got to be doubly sure we're keeping the POW wives in line. Is there anything you can think of that needs to be done at this point?

On April 29, 1971, General Hughes responded in a memo to Haldeman:

Subject: POW/MIA WIVES

You are aware of my increasing concern about purely PR therapy being effective for much longer. Nevertheless, after a meeting with Al Haig and Chuck Colson, I feel that increased efforts in the "cosmetic" area are warranted and indeed essential to keep the families with us during the critical period of the next six to eight weeks. In addition to personal daily contact with the National League of Families in a continuing effort to show our concern... here are some of the other activities we plan. [The list of activities included a presidential press conference, a meeting by Henry Kissinger with the Board of Directors of the National League of Families, a speech by the vice-president ("it may be that the president ...should pre-empt him"), an effort to arrange a television appearance by the League's National Coordinator, and an appearance on the "Today Show" by a high-ranking Pentagon official who "did a superb job of upholding the administration's position and setting the POW/MIA matter in proper perspective."]

According to Al Haig, the next eight weeks are critical and the efforts of the Ad Hoc Coordinating Group on POW/MIA Matters will be devoted to keeping the families on the reservation in order to buy this time.

Brigadier General James D. Hughes

The cynical words in the memoranda made me feel very sad. But I was not surprised. *Thank God we kept hammering away*, I thought. I was also thankful that I hadn't seen these memoranda at the time they were written. I probably would have thrown up my hands in defeat.

"That's just the way they do things, I guess," Red said. "They were still 'handling' the League of Families in 1979 and 1980, long after the war ended."

He handed me four more sheets of paper, memoranda from the Carter White House. One of the memos expressed concern that an American "defector," Bobby Garwood, was "on his way home" and that "his return will generate new stories...about the possibility that additional Americans remain in Hanoi." The writer of the memo, National Security Council staffer Michel Oksenberg, stated his view that "it would be *politically wise* [italics mine] for the president to indicate his own continued concern with the MIAs...since the Administration had implied earlier that it believed Vietnamese assurances that there were no live Americans left in Hanoi."

Oksenberg was the writer of two more memoranda which referred to requests by the National League of Families to meet with National Security Council Advisor Zbigniew Brzezinski. In one he recommended that Brzezinski "indicate that you take recent refugee reports of sighting of live prisoners 'seriously.' This is simply good politics; DIA (Defense Intelligence Agency) and State are *playing this game* [italics mine], and you should not be the whistle-blower. The idea is to say that the president is determined to pursue any lead concerning possible live MIAs...Apparently you revealed skepticism..., and my recommended letter to the League *walks you back from that* [italics mine]."

In the other memo, Oksenberg stated that "the League is increasingly convinced Vietnam holds live Americans in Vietnam" and recommended that "As 1980 [election year] approaches, we must redouble our efforts to maintain liaison with such organizations."

The last of the four memos was from Brzezinski to President Carter.

"The National League of Families remains convinced that live American POWs remain in Vietnam. They also believe you are not being adequately informed and that the bureaucracy is not pursuing the matter aggressively..."

I slowly handed the stack of papers back to the young reporter.

"You keep them," he said. "They show an ongoing effort to keep the POW issue under wraps. But they've gotten more sophisticated now. They've co-opted the League leadership somehow."

The other young man nodded his agreement.

"Not only that," he said, "but there's an organized campaign to smear anyone who asks any questions. It's called intimidation."

"Oh, come on!" I protested. "These memos just show how the political game is played. At least the National League made itself important enough that White House memos went back and forth about us. I think we knew that. But a smear campaign? That's really paranoid."

"Well, if you and Captain McDaniel get into it, you'll find out," the young man said, getting to his feet. "And I have a feeling the captain's about to jump in with both feet."

Red walked them to the door and then came back to his desk, picking up the papers I had set down there.

"What do you think, Dorothy?"

"Oh, I'm not surprised. I think I always knew this was the way it was done. Whenever they thought we might get out of line, the White House would send the president to talk to us. It worked every time," I said.

"And I think they're still doing the same thing in the Reagan White House. But I don't see how they could *co-opt* a family member. During the war, most of the families were easily persuaded by the rhetoric, and some of the leaders were impressed by being invited to the White House, getting to meet personally with the president and Kissinger. That always worked pretty well. We called it the 'Rose Garden Strategy.' But co-opted is a pretty strong word! And using intimidation? I just don't know about that."

"Yeah, that's pretty farfetched," Red nodded. "That boy has been trying to get information about his dad for *twelve years!* I guess you imagine all kinds of things after that length of time. But, you know, he's collected a lot of stuff. Some of it is pretty scary," he said, and he didn't elaborate.

"He's about Mike's age, Red," I said. "That could be one of our children, if you hadn't made it back."

He looked at me steadily.

"It *would* have been one of ours," he said pointedly, "if you wives hadn't put the fear of God into those guys in the White House."

I could see that the memos from two administrations had made him very angry. They undermined his belief that, in America, things were done for the right reasons.

"I wonder what the memos in the Reagan White House say," he continued slowly, gathering up the papers and adding them to the growing POW file on his desk. "It may be time to start asking some questions."

He was deeply troubled by the suggestion that there was an official effort to discredit those who asked questions about the government's handling of POW information. A former director of the Defense Intelligence Agency, General Eugene Tighe, had stated publicly that there was a great deal of evidence that Americans were still being held, and that officials had a "mind-set to debunk" such evidence. But "debunk" was one thing; to purposely intimidate was something else. Red couldn't believe his government was capable of *that!*

Then Red himself became a target. He started asking the troubling questions publicly. And when he did, all hell broke loose for him. It started around midnight one hot summer evening in 1985. Both Red and I were awakened by the insistent ringing of the phone on the table by Red's side of the bed.

"Red, this is Dick Childress at the White House," a garrulous voice boomed.

I had never met Colonel Dick Childress, but Red had told me about him. I knew he handled POW matters at the National Security Council. Red had told me earlier in the evening that he had seen Colonel Childress at the annual POW/MIA families' meeting that day and that he appeared to be acting as "stage manager," as if he were running the meeting behind the scene.

"It must be his job to placate the families," Red had commented to me when he came home from the meeting.

"You mean 'keep them on the reservation,'" I said. "Remember the memos from the Nixon White House and the Carter White House? About keeping the families in line?"

It was becoming obvious to both of us that Dick Childress had fallen heir to the task of keeping the families in line and on the reservation.

Childress' voice was so loud coming out of the telephone receiver in Red's hand that I could hear it distinctly from my side of our king-sized bed. It didn't sound very friendly. Clearly, the call was to let Red know the White House didn't like the questions Red had raised at the family meeting about refugee sightings of live Americans in captivity and about how the White House was dealing with such reports.

Groggy with sleep, Red held the receiver a few inches from his ear and just listened, puzzled. Finally, he asked, "Tell me, Dick, do you think we still have American POWs in Southeast Asia?"

"You're damn right we do," Colonel Dick Childress of the White House staff boomed.

Red bolted upright in bed, wide awake now.

"When do we get them home, Dick?" he asked.

"In two or three years, Red."

"That's too long, Dick. They're running out of time," Red said and hung up the receiver.

We were mystified. The purpose of Childress' call was clearly to intimidate, to get Red to back off. After all, it was the White House calling! Red was infuriated by the implications of the call. But he was also elated.

"The White House just confirmed that our government *knows* some of the guys are still over there!" he yelled.

"But why don't they say so publicly? Why try to hide it?" I pondered.

"Who knows?" he answered. "Maybe they're ashamed of it. They oughta be.

"What I don't understand is the two or three years part. My God, we're talking about *men!* We're talking about men who've been locked up for twelve, fifteen years. They can't wait two or three more years! They'll be dead," he protested.

"That's true. In two or three years the problem will resolve itself. They'll all be dead. And we won't have to worry about how to get them out," I said sarcastically.

His eyes widened.

"And in two or three years, Ronald Reagan won't have to deal with it," I continued, mercilessly. "This is 1985. Reagan's last year is 1988. Maybe he'll bring them home just before election day."

"Or maybe people will forget about it," he replied. "We just can't let that happen!"

Red rolled over and pulled the blanket up to his chin. I lay still, staring at the ceiling. I was frightened by Childress' call—and by Red's reaction to it. *He won't be intimidated. He'll wake up tomorrow morning more determined than ever. But what will all of this do to him?* He came home from Vietnam with his body and soul intact, his spirit unbroken. He loved his country. He believed in his country. He fought his battles. He fought his country's battles in a faraway land. Now he was being forced to do battle with people who are supposed to be his friends. I was frightened for him. I was also very angry. *He doesn't deserve this, not at the hands of his friends, his own country. Not by those in the Reagan White House, of all people.*

It was almost dawn. I got out of bed and went over to the window, tiptoeing to keep from awakening Red. He had an early morning appointment; he needed his sleep.

But he wasn't asleep.

"I believed in Ronald Reagan," he said quietly. "I know he cared about POWs. I know he sent some teams in there back in 1981 to get some guys out. I can't believe he would abandon them."

I got back into bed.

"Red, there's no telling what they tell Reagan. This is a democracy remember? And in a democracy the biggest fires are the ones that get put out. Childress' job is to keep the POW fire under control."

"You're right. It's a democracy. And in a democracy every man counts. Even if he's a long-lost, emaciated POW, he *counts*. We're not just talking about POWs here. We're talking about national honor," he said angrily. "You can't just sweep people under the rug. You can't just pretend they don't exist. You can't just abandon men who went into battle at their country's call when they fall into enemy hands. You can't call men expendable, like tanks, guns, and aircraft. They're *men!* You just can't do it. It would destroy a nation!"

"But you can't fight every battle, Red. This isn't your job. Why are you making this *your* job?"

First daylight had broken, and I could see his face. There were tears in his eyes.

"Because it's the right thing to do," he said sadly.

19

The Unseen Enemy

The battle for the POWs America left behind in Southeast Asia was, Red said, the toughest battle of his life.

"I can't figure out who the enemy is," Red told his old squadron mate and good friend, Bruce Richards. The three of us were leaving the POW/MIA families' board meeting one crisp fall day in 1985. "B.R." had flown down from Boston, where he practiced law, to go with us to the meeting. We were trying to figure out why the POW/MIA family group wasn't pressing harder to get the POWs home, and we hoped B.R. could help us determine their motives.

Red was on the board of directors of the National League of Families, and the meetings were becoming unbearable for him. Ann Mills Griffiths, the executive director who ran the meetings, opposed anyone who questioned the organization's position: that the League fully supported the Reagan administration's handling of the POW issue. Recently, Ann had begun attacking Red in the League of Families' newsletter and in speeches she gave as the POW families' official representative, some of which were shown on national television.

"Fighting her is like fighting apple pie and motherhood," B.R. commented as we left the meeting. "She's a family member."

"By the way, Dorothy, didn't you help organize that group?" he asked, turning to me.

"Yes, and when and if we ever get another prisoner home, I'll have to apologize to him for the inactivity and downright opposition of the group I helped organize," I said. "I have to apologize now to Red for the personal attacks on him by the very organization that helped bring him home. It's incredible!"

I told him about meeting in Washington with a small group of POW/MIA family members from all over the country in 1970.

"We were an ad hoc committee to formalize the National League of Families, to give cohesion to our scattered efforts to focus attention on our husbands and sons during the war. The League was a strong advocacy group in the years following the war, keeping their cause before the public, putting pressure on our government to find out about the men who were still missing. Red, the memos from the Carter White House show how effective they were. When all those refugees reported seeing Americans in captivity, the League continued to be a force that had to be dealt with. Then, after Reagan was elected, somehow the League became an arm of the government. I don't know how or why," I said.

"I don't know, either," Red chimed in. "But I do know the National League is becoming an obstacle to getting prisoners home. Members of Congress who don't want to get involved hide behind the League, saying the families are content with government policy. Those who do want to get involved are afraid the League will attack them if they don't say the 'right' thing. As B.R. just said, disagreeing with the POW/MIA family members is like disagreeing with apple pie and motherhood. Politicians can't afford to do that. It just isn't good politics to get into this issue in any meaningful way anymore. The National League has seen to that. All the families that contact me have left the National League of Families in dismay. And the League attacks the dissident families as much as it does me."

B.R. was on the board of directors at the American Defense Institute as well as being one of the best sounding boards Red had. After dinner that night, he and Red sat out on our back porch in the deep twilight and talked about ways the Institute could help get the POW issue on the front burner in Washington.

"National defense is what we're all about at ADI," Red said. "I believe that any country's defense depends a great deal on the mo-

rale of the fighting man. And every time I speak to a group of servicemen and women, or to a group that has any service personnel
in it, for that matter, they ask when we're going to bring the rest of
our POWs home. I never bring it up. I talk about military voting,
or just give a motivational speech using my POW experiences,
when I'm talking to a military audience. I never talk about the
POW issue. It shouldn't be their problem; there's not much they
can do about it. But they always ask. They believe we left men behind when we left Southeast Asia. And it bothers them," he said.
"It bothers them a lot."

"You're right, Red," B.R. agreed. "It isn't their problem. It's
ours. And what you just said makes it a national defense problem.
So ADI should be into it," he said.

I could hear their conversation from the kitchen, where I was
putting the dinner dishes into the dishwasher. I walked over to the
open door to the porch and reminded them of the student programs at ADI.

"And think about the young people," I said. "We're teaching
them patriotism, how to love and to serve their country. How can
we ask them to serve their country if their country may abandon
them if we have to send them into combat some day?"

"Dorothy, I pray that we never have to send any more young
Americans into combat again," Red said through the open door.
"But I know we probably will. It's a dangerous world, and we'll always have to fight freedom's battles. We will have to ask them to
go, and they'll go willingly. It's up to us to make sure our country is
behind them when they go.

"One of the lessons the nation learned from the Vietnam experience is this: Don't commit the troops unless the nation itself is
committed. Another lesson I hope we learned is to go into battle
to *win* or don't go at all!"

I had walked out onto the porch and sat down in one of the
deck chairs.

"I hope you're wrong, Red," I said, "I mean about the inevita-
bility of future wars. But if you're right, future wars mean more
POWs. I'd like to believe that the efforts of the POW/MIA families
during the Vietnam War will in some small way help POW/MIA
families in the future—and guarantee the nation's commitment to

bring all the POWs home when the war ends. Surely the public debate about those who didn't come home after Vietnam will make sure we never leave any behind again."

B.R. nodded thoughtfully.

"There's no doubt about it. The American people will see to that. And, Dorothy, I'd be willing to wager that no congressman will ever again say to a POW wife what that one guy said to you about the Vietnamese being justified in their refusal to treat POWs with humanity."

"Oh, you mean the congressman who said we couldn't very well make a big deal about the Red Cross and the mail as long as we were bombing?"

"Yep," B.R. replied. "Mark my words, you'll hear a lot about the Geneva Conventions the next time an American pilot goes down."

I shuddered. I didn't want to think about another pilot going down, ever. The next time it would be naval aviators who had attended the Naval Academy with Mike and had spent so many weekends in our home while they were midshipmen. Or it would be some of the wonderful young people who had worked and studied at the American Defense Institute. Or our own little grandsons.

"Why can't nations learn to live together in peace?" I said aloud. "Maybe we've learned that. Maybe we won't have another war."

"You're talking like a grandmother, Dorothy. None of us want...," B.R. began.

"I *am* a grandmother!" I interrupted.

"What I started to say," B.R. continued patiently, "is that none of us want war. ADI is working for peace by advocating a strong defense so the enemies of freedom will think twice before starting anything. But we'll have another war the next time some bully somewhere in the world wants to take away someone else's freedom. We've always had to fight for freedom, and we always will."

Red joined in.

"B.R., did I ever tell you about the sign I saw when I first came home and went to speak on an Ivy League campus at the same time some students were demonstrating against the draft? It was printed on a bedsheet hanging from a dormitory window, and it said, 'Nothing is worth dying for.' I've thought a lot about that sign. We don't want young Americans to die, but we do want them to know there are things worth fighting for—and dying for, if necessary. Freedom's one of them."

He should know, I thought. *He knows how it feels to lose his freedom.*

"I know; you're right," I said. "But it breaks my heart to think of other families going through what we went through, what Mike, David, and Leslie went through for six years, growing up without a father, having their mother neglect them to fight for their dad, all of that."

"It won't be six years the next time, Dorothy," B.R. replied. "We won't leave them there for six, seven, eight years the next time. And we won't abandon some of them the next time. That's one reason it's so important to keep talking about those we left behind in Vietnam. And that's why ADI should be into it; that's why it's a national defense problem."

"Yes, it is," I said, relieved to be back in the present. "Let's stop talking about future wars and decide if we can afford to risk ADI's future by adding the POW issue to the agenda. Red has built that organization with blood, sweat, and tears, you know."

Red had been reluctant to involve ADI in his battle for the POWs. He didn't want to jeopardize the organization. Yet he knew that the nation's defense depended on the morale of the nation's fighting forces. And morale depended on the fighting forces' trust in their leaders. If someone didn't find a resolution to the POW issue, and soon, it could explode into a major scandal that would destroy the one thing that gave the United States an edge over her enemies: superior troop morale.

Red knew he couldn't win the battle by himself. He needed to use the resources of the American Defense Institute. This approach made sense to many of his supporters, who believed in what he was trying to do for the POWs.

"You're right, B.R.," he said. "We've laid everything else on the line. We'll put ADI out there, too."

A few weeks later, Red spoke to a group of students at Flagler College in St. Augustine, Florida. In answer to one of their questions about the POW issue, he made reference to an article published in the *Boston Globe* criticizing the official in charge of POW/MIA affairs at the Pentagon. A month after he returned from Florida, Red received a letter from a Washington attorney representing that official, warning him to speak only the truth about his client in the Pentagon. The message was clear.

"We're watching you wherever you go. We're listening to everything you say. Be careful."

"Big Brother is watching us, Red," I suggested.

We soon wondered if our phones were being monitored as well. But Red was philosophical about such a possibility.

"We don't have any secrets. Perhaps we're making a small dent in the bureaucratic wall. Otherwise, why would they bother to keep tabs on us?"

But to be on the safe side, we started keeping a log and making tape recorded records of our activities, so the story would survive if we didn't. I was working full-time at ADI, and every night as we drove down the George Washington Parkway, through Old Town, and along the Potomac River toward Mount Vernon, Red would relate the events of his day to me while I held the tape recorder. Then we sent the tapes to an out-of-town friend for safekeeping. She was really spooked when we told her what to do with the tapes if anything should happen to us.

The decision to work on the POW issue at ADI brought an onslaught of criticism. Newsletters from the National League of Families questioned Red's motives in pursuing the POW issue. Opponents on Capitol Hill called for an investigation of ADI. Even the Defense Intelligence Agency joined the fray, circulating a letter which called Red "less than candid."

Destroying Red McDaniel's credibility was difficult. It's hard to convince others that a man decorated with medals like the Navy Cross and the Silver Star, and a chestful of other honors, is a liar. After a man has been selected for some of the Navy's most critical leadership roles, the claim that he's not to be trusted is not believable.

Many of the attacks used similar language, causing us to wonder if the smear campaign was being orchestrated by one person behind the scenes. It was scary to think that something like this could happen in the United States of America, to a man who had served his country with distinction for twenty-seven years, almost dying in a communist prisoner of war camp.

"I can't believe anyone really swallows all those lies," Monika Jensen said to Red, referring to the attacks on him and on many others like him who refused to stop asking questions about the POWs.

Monika and her writer husband, Bill Stevenson, were writing a book about the government's abandonment of the POWs. Red was helping them, letting them use the tapes he had made and putting them in contact with POW activists around the country. Monika's research for the book had brought her into contact with many victims of the opposition's smear tactics.

"It's like a Soviet disinformation campaign," she continued. "It's definitely being directed from behind the scenes. And you're not being paranoid. People have been *killed* for trying to expose this issue."

"Well, it's a free country," Red responded. "And I have the right to believe POWs are still in Southeast Asia—and to say I believe it. Even if they aren't there—and they *are*—even if they aren't there, I have the right to believe they are. And I have the right to *say* I believe they are still there.

"This issue is bigger than POWs. It's about national honor. And it's about freedom!"

He had lost his freedom in a foreign land and had regained it when he came home in 1973. He was determined now to make use of the freedom in his own country to speak out for the men we left behind—to try to restore *their* freedom.

The attacks on ADI didn't work. Too many people agreed with Red and understood the tragic implications for our nation of the betrayal of our POWs. POW/MIA family members who felt that they, too, had been betrayed by their own leaders looked to us to keep the issue alive.

Red was meticulous about recording the money that people contributed to ADI for the POW awareness effort, making sure that none of it was ever used for any other ADI program. The audit performed at the end of every year showed that other ADI funds had to be used to subsidize the POW program. We even had to use some of our personal funds to pay for POW awareness expenses. But the opposition accused us of being involved with the POW issue for "personal gain." Now we understood how the intimidation campaign worked: Say something derogatory about someone—you don't have to prove it, just say it and you arouse suspicion to undermine the integrity of your opponent.

It would have been so easy to quit. It was an uphill battle all the way, and the opposition was fierce. It was almost impossible to see any progress, but we knew that each passing day was a "life or death" day for the men in the POW camps.

I kept thinking, *I've done all this before. Why am I having to do it again?*

The worst part was what it was doing to Red. I could see his disillusionment. He had survived six years as a prisoner of war because of his absolute faith in God—and in his country. Now the core of his faith in his country was being shaken. His enemies were a small group of people. Yet that small group seemed to have enough power to use the agencies of our government for their own ends. He had always said, "My country right or wrong." Now he knew his country would be wrong if a few powerful bureaucrats in Washington were allowed to abandon servicemen to their fate in God-forsaken prisons on the other side of the world.

"Help us in our decisions," he beseeched the Lord daily.

And I prayed that Red's faith in God would remain steadfast. It was dangerous, I knew, to confuse faith in God and faith in country.

*   *   *

ADI sponsored several campaigns to focus attention on the POWs and offered a reward, payable to any citizen of Vietnam, Laos, or Cambodia who would defect and bring an American POW home to freedom. The reward money was pledged by congressmen and ordinary citizens, the pledges to be paid when a POW was free. We made a major effort to advertise the reward offer in the United States and throughout Southeast Asia. The campaign was called

"Home Free!" and its value was in the attention that it focused on the POWs. We knew the men would not come home until the U.S. government decided to get serious about negotiating for them, and we knew those negotiations would not happen until the American people demanded it. But we also thought there was a slim chance of getting one or two of the men out with the reward offer. If we could, then it would be easy to rally public opinion to get the rest.

At the same time, ADI and ADF were experiencing growing pains. We were trying to produce as many programs for students as possible with limited staff and limited space. Our membership had grown to over 100,000. People from all walks of life believed in what we were doing for young people, and they wanted to help.

Red was speaking all over the country, and he had enlisted other speakers with special appeal to young people to help meet the increasing demand. The word was spreading on college campuses about the student internships and fellowships at ADI, and we had to turn down many students who wanted to come to Washington to learn about government and defense policymaking.

ADF was establishing a base on Capitol Hill, building on the personal contacts Red had made while he was still in the Navy as Capitol Hill liaison, and the organization was having an influence on some of the key defense votes.

It was almost impossible to keep up with all the activity. Since we couldn't pay large salaries, we had high turnover on the staff. Only the dedicated ones lasted, the ones who were truly committed to the effort and could afford to make the sacrifice. It wasn't a place for the faint-hearted. Everyone was doing the jobs of two people and, even then, we couldn't keep up. Most of our staff were part of the "under-thirty crowd," and they amazed us with their energy and dedication.

In 1984, ADI had organized a military voter registration program, to register and encourage service personnel to vote. This program was rapidly becoming another force for freedom and was one of the programs at ADI that Red was most proud of. The program had received a lot of attention in Washington and had gained the support of members of Congress from both political parties and from the White House.

When Red spoke on military bases, he talked about his experience as a POW. He admitted to them that he had never voted when he left for Vietnam at age thirty-five.

"I didn't think it was important for a military man to vote. He was just supposed to follow orders. But I learned to appreciate the right to vote. Voting is not just a right; it's a responsibility."

Service personnel were not encouraged to vote for any particular candidate or political party. Red's message to them about voting dealt primarily with their right—and their obligation—to exercise the rights they had sworn to defend for other citizens.

"Those who fight—and sometimes die—for democracy must also *vote* for democracy," Red said in his speech to Army troops stationed in Frankfurt, Germany, in the summer of 1984. These young soldiers would not be at their polling places on election day, and they needed to be convinced of the importance of their individual votes and begin early the somewhat complicated process of voting by absentee ballot.

"You know, you're not a constituency for any of the politicians," he continued. "When our lawmakers see a need to slash the defense budget, the first place they look is at military pay and allowances and veterans' benefits. That's because members of the armed services don't vote. In a democracy it's the *voters* who make policy. That's another reason for military personnel—and veterans—to vote."

Although Red had come home to a hero's welcome, as had all the POWs, other veterans from Vietnam had not been welcomed so warmly. Many of them felt that they had to apologize for serving in such an unpopular war, and the politicians weren't very interested in legislation to provide new veterans' benefits.

The nation's lack of concern for the returning troops, who sometimes had to slink back and try to lose their identity as Vietnam veterans, was troubling to Red and the American Defense Institute and one of the motivating factors for ADI's Military Voter Program.

"Pay and allowances and veterans' benefits have a big effect on military morale," he told those who were interested in supporting the effort to register military voters. "They certainly didn't join the service to get rich; they'll probably always be underpaid for what they do. But they need to be appreciated, and when no one is interested in their pay and benefits, it shows a lack of appreciation, and it definitely lowers morale.

"The next war will be fought by an all-volunteer force. The high-tech weapons and sophisticated hardware which we'll have to use will require men and women who are highly motivated, well-trained, and professional. We need to attract young people of high caliber who will want to excel."

"Red, how do you know that the military voter will vote the way we want him to?" one of the ADI directors asked at the 1984 board meeting.

"We don't; some of them are probably super-liberal," was Red's answer. "But that's okay. We still want them to exercise their right to vote, don't we? We want them to know they count, that they're not second-class citizens because they're in the military.

"We'll have to take a chance on how they vote. That's what democracy's all about: taking a chance on how people vote. However, I think most of our servicemen and women want an adequate defense budget, don't you? They don't want to go into combat with outdated, inferior equipment. And they surely want to take care of their families. Some of *Lexington's* enlisted men worked at McDonald's at night and on weekends, when they needed to be home with their wives and kids. They made more money at McDonald's than they did in the Navy, and that's wrong!"

He's talking about the next war again, I thought. *The next time we go into combat. And everyone seems to agree with him that there'll be a next time. It's not inevitable, is it?*

My worry about Red's being bitter about the seven years of his life he had given to the losing cause in Vietnam had proved to be unfounded. Saigon had fallen in 1975 during his command of *Niagara Falls* and he had wept in front of the TV when he saw South Vietnamese citizens desperately trying to hang onto the wings of the aircraft evacuating personnel from the beleaguered American Embassy. He had realized soon after his return that the nation's will to provide financial assistance to the Thieu government would be short-lived, and he knew democracy in South Vietnam could not survive without it. Watergate had undermined the political power President Nixon needed to persuade Congress to appropriate the funds, and Congress was ready to forget the war and the American sacrifice and move on to other, more politically attractive, budget items.

"How can they just let all that sacrifice go down the drain?" I protested. "After spilling all that blood, how in God's name can we not at least give dollars? For a little while longer, anyway."

"The people don't have the will to do it," Red replied. "It proves my point: don't commit the troops until the nation is committed. We learned that in Vietnam if we didn't learn anything else."

He paused.

"We learned a lot of lessons in Vietnam, Dorothy. At least, I hope we learned them. If we did learn them, and we don't forget them, then the sacrifices will count for something. It's up to those of us who made the sacrifices to make sure the nation doesn't forget the lessons...because you know *we* aren't going to forget the lessons!"

Yes, I knew we wouldn't forget the lessons we had learned. Red had completed *Scars and Stripes*, the book about his POW experience, just before the toppling of the Saigon government, and the reliving of his life in the Hanoi Hilton had made him more aware that he had learned some personal lessons as well as some lessons for his country.

"I learned to appreciate freedom," he told me, "and I learned to appreciate you and the children. I took those things pretty much for granted before. It may be that you have to have things like that taken away from you in order to know their value.

"I learned that a man can take away everything you possess— your clothes, your food, your health, even your freedom—but he can't destroy your will to survive and he can't destroy your will to believe. He can't destroy your faith.

"I learned another very important truth: courage is not the absence of fear. I was scared to death in that torture room. Courage is not the absence of fear; courage is simply the presence of faith."

I had learned my lessons well, too, I hoped. Like the refiner's fire, my suffering had made me a better person—thankful, compassionate, committed to the things that really count. I knew I would never again be complacent, nor take my blessings for granted.

When others suffered, I would feel their pain in my own heart. I would greet each new day as an opportunity, I hoped—and as a gift from God.

*   *   *

As Red travelled to military bases around the world, encouraging the armed forces to vote, he became even more acutely aware of the need to resolve the POW issue. From the questions the servicemen asked, he decided it was common knowledge among the troops that all the POWs had not come home when the war in Vietnam ended. He knew his stubborn refusal to drop the POW issue was jeopardizing his work at the American Defense Institute, consuming time, energy and resources that were needed for other efforts. It was making him very unpopular in some quarters in the nation's capital. But he was convinced that, if he could somehow bypass the bureaucracy and get President Reagan's ear, the president would act to bring the men home. He met with Nancy Reynolds, a personal friend of the Reagans. He talked at length with Lyn Nofziger, the president's lifelong political advisor. He briefed Jerry Denton and John McCain, former POWs who now served in Congress, as well as many other members of Congress he had worked with on the Hill during his Navy liaison days. He talked with his friend Ross Perot, and he knew that Perot had met with Reagan to discuss the POWs. When he was invited to appear at a New York fundraiser with Secretary of the Treasury Jim Baker, he flew with Secretary Baker to New York and back and gave him all the information he had about the POWs.

At every opportunity, Red pleaded with those in positions of power to conduct an investigation into the handling of POW evidence. Early one Saturday morning he received a call from a retired Air Force general, a covert operations specialist who wanted to help Red get through to Reagan.

"Red," he said, "I have a friend who is a speechwriter for Reagan. He's meeting with the president this morning and has agreed to ask him about the POWs. He's leaving the White House to run for Congress in California, and today is his last meeting with the president. Let's go talk to him. Can you meet me at the White House in thirty minutes?"

Red threw on his clothes, jumped in the car, and raced down the Parkway to Washington to the Old Executive Office Building, where he and his Air Force friend met Dana Rohrabacher, the president's speechwriter.

"I have five minutes with the president, Red," Dana said. "If you had one request of the president, what would you ask him to do?"

Red thought for a moment. Five minutes wasn't long enough to convince the president that some of the POWs were alive and waiting for rescue. Anyway, he knew the president had known that at one time. Reagan had ordered some rescue missions to recover POWs early in his administration. Probably the best thing to do was to get him to appoint a commission to look into the evidence. He knew Reagan knew and respected Ross Perot. A commission headed by Perot would take an independent look at the evidence. A commission headed by Perot would bring prisoners home. He was sure of it.

"Tell the president this," Red said. "Tell him to create a victory for Ronald Reagan by bringing prisoners home. Ask him to appoint Ross Perot to head a presidential commission to look into the evidence that POWs are still alive. I don't see how anyone could object to *that*."

"Wait here and I'll tell you what he says," Dana suggested.

In a few minutes, the speechwriter returned.

"It worked, Red," he said. "The president is very concerned. He suggested that you call Judge William Clark, his former National Security Advisor, and ask him to call Ross Perot to talk about it."

"He wants me to call him? Why doesn't he call him? I'm not sure I can get through to Judge Clark."

"I don't know, Red. But that's what he said," Dana responded.

"Well, I'll sure give it a try. Thanks, Dana."

On Monday Red called Judge William Clark's office and left a message. The next day he heard that Judge Clark had been injured in an aircraft accident, so he decided to wait to try again. A few weeks later, he tried again, but Judge Clark never returned his calls. On the outside chance that Reagan might follow up himself, Red checked with Ross Perot. But Perot had not heard from the president or from Judge Clark.

"I'm not going to get appointed to any commission, Red," Perot said. "There're too many people who don't want anybody taking an independent look."

Texas businessman Ross Perot was as convinced as Red that some of the POWs had been left behind, and he was still working behind the scenes to bring some of them home. He and Red agreed that it would eventually take U.S. government commitment to negotiate for them, but that one or two freed men would help prove that the rest of them were there. One or two freed men would bring pressure on government officials to secure the others' release.

"If we can just get one living, breathing, skinny American out, we can rally the nation to demand the rest," Red had said to the ADI staff when he first told them about the plans to offer a reward.

I was grateful for Ross Perot. Every time Red talked with him, which was often, he came away upbeat and optimistic. Perot was a man who didn't have to care, but he did, and he cared very deeply. If anyone could make it happen, Perot could.

Red knew Perot would keep working to get the men home. He himself would continue to try and reach as many influential people as he could. But he had come to the conclusion that it would be grassroots America who would finally get the job done.

"You were right, Dorothy," he said. "In Washington, the biggest fires are the ones that get put out. We're just going to have to build the biggest fire we can. The POWs will come home when the American people demand it."

Somehow, he had to uncover the evidence that American servicemen were still in captivity—and show it to the American people. But he knew now that his unseen enemy would go to any length to keep that from happening.

20

They Were My Children...

L eslie had worked off and on at ADI all through college. She joined her dad's staff permanently in 1987. She had grown up without him and it had been hard for her to learn to love him when he came home. But a letter she wrote to Red when she came to work for him at ADI told him all he needed to know:

Dear Dad,

I am writing to you because of a strong need I have to tell you how I feel. It is awkward to write a letter to you, but there is so much inside of me that I want to communicate to you that requires deep thought as to the best way to tell you.

First and foremost, I thank you with all that I am for all that you represent. Your life exemplifies the ultimate human sacrifice for what you know to be right. You pursue righteousness, whatever the cost.

I want to work with you at the American Defense Institute primarily because of what you mean to me as a father. I never fully appreciated you as I was growing up, I believe because of your absence in my life from the age of four until I was ten. Then upon your return, I remember thinking that I was supposed to love you, but I didn't. I didn't know you, and here you were, a stranger in my secure little world. As I moved into my selfish adolescent years, I sensed your strength as a great man, but I saw you as a lot of teen-agers see their parents, an obstacle to freedom and fun.

It wasn't until I left home and went away to college that I really be-gan to understand just how fortunate I am to have the parents I have. Your faithfulness and gentleness as a father and a husband became apparent to me. I became so proud of you and all that you are. When you ran for Congress while I was in college, I took a se-mester off to come help because I wanted to show you how much I loved you.

What I didn't realize was that I carried a lot of guilt for not allow-ing you to be a real father to me after you came home from Viet-nam. It wasn't until I went to see the movie *Hanoi Hilton* with a friend that I saw myself as tremendously selfish for not allowing you into my world. My friend and I went out for coffee after the movie and we were discussing your experiences as a POW. I began to share how badly I felt for not letting you love me when you came home. My friend said, "But you were a ten-year-old little girl. You didn't think then as an adult, as you do now. You thought like a child, because you were a child!" Believe it or not, that conversation radically changed the way I see my relationship with you. I began to relate to you out of a sense of love and respect rather than a sense of duty.

I want to work with you again because I have come to appreciate you as so much more than a father: a great leader of men, who puts all he has—career, reputation and life—on the line for causes he knows to be right. In a day when men sell their souls for their careers, at the expense of anyone in the way, I have a father who stands alone!

I am learning from you many things that are making me into the woman God has designed me to be. You are my earthly picture of what my Heavenly Father represents. I thank you from the bot-tom of my heart for all that you are. You are my hero and I love you, Leslie.

Leslie's letter meant a great deal to Red—and to me. She couldn't know his love in her early years, so the love she had for him now was a love growing out of her admiration for the work he was doing, for the kind of man he was; fearless, undaunted, deter-mined to take the right course, regardless of the cost.

It was good to have one of our children close to home and working with us at ADI. Mike and Deb lived in California with little Michael and Daryl. Michael was born on my fiftieth birth-day, which I thought was very appropriate. Red's release occurred in March of 1973, a few days before my fortieth. Then my first grandchild was born on my fiftieth.(I can't wait to see what happens in March 1993, when I turn sixty.)

Mike had graduated from the Naval Academy and served as an engineer on a destroyer home-ported in San Diego. After his two little boys were born, he decided to leave the Navy. I think he remembered how it was to have his dad away while he was growing up, and he didn't want Michael and Daryl to grow up without their dad around. But he continued to serve in the Naval Reserves. He was a Navy man, through and through, and couldn't bring himself to leave it completely. He joined a San Diego consulting firm that provided oversight for Navy ship repair and overhauls, a perfect job for a former Navy engineer and one which offered a bright future.

He and Deb were settling down in San Diego. I sometimes wished Red and I could relocate to California so we could see our grandchildren grow up. We'd also be near Dave, who had married Joni, the love of his life, and settled down in San Diego. (In 1989, Dave and Joni presented us with our third grandchild, Christopher, a cute little replica of his granddad, and early in 1991, our fourth—Kyle Charles.)

Dave, the little seven-year-old who had fought Red's battles with plastic soldiers on the family-room floor, had grown up to be the family entrepreneur. After fighting the battle for the congressional seat with Red, Dave went back to finish college and then went west to start his own business. Fiercely independent, he combined his love of the ocean with his business sense and sold beachwear and other beach items in his own store at the edge of the Pacific.

When I first saw Dave's shop overlooking the ocean, I remembered the poem he had written when he was in high school:

Perched high on a cliff by the sea
I feel overwhelmingly free;
So far away are the troubles and worries
Of city life hassles and everyday hurries;
I feel overwhelmingly free.
Relaxed by the sounds of the ocean,

I ponder the infinite motion
Of waves pounding the shore,
And seagulls as they soar.
I ponder the infinite motion.

Absorbed by the power and beauty,
I wish it were my only duty
To sit on this cliff overlooking the sea
With nothing to do and nowhere to be.
I wish it were my only duty.

Leslie was engaged to Jim Lindsay, a young minister who had come to Alexandria to work with the youth in our church.* She and Jim began to develop a unique music ministry which is their special contribution to today's youth. Leslie's rapport with teenagers is, I believe, the result of her own painful growing up.

All three of our children had found their niches, and their life-mates. Life had been tough for them, but the hard times had given Mike, David, and Leslie a special strength, and a deep love for one another.

Every Christmas our growing family would gather in our home in Alexandria. It was a long way to come, but they always came. Sometimes we would get out the reels of television footage of Red's return from Hanoi, watch ourselves in tenuous reunion, and relive some of the hurt—and all of the joy.

Other times Red would get out his purple-and-gray striped pajama-like prison uniform, the one he wore for six years as a POW. He would re-tell the stories of Christmas in Hanoi, how the POWs would improvise a tree from green socks and white bandages and give one another imaginary gifts. On Christmas Day, he never failed to put on the ragged red woolen socks, the ones we had mailed to Hanoi in 1969. He called them his "miracle socks." His captors had decided that year to allow him to have the bottle of multi-vitamins in the package and, wonder of wonders, the red socks! His captors had decided that year to allow him to have the bottle of multi-vitamins in the package and, wonder of wonders, the red socks!

Red never would tell us how he managed to smuggle these and other personal items—his tin cup, his metal spoon, his worn black

---

*Leslie and Jim were married in 1990, and Leslie continues to work at the American Defense Institute.

rubber sandals crudely fashioned from an old tire—out of Vietnam when he was released. Most of the contraband was now on loan to the Naval Aviation Museum in Pensacola, but he kept the red socks and the striped pajamas as "reminders," he said, "of my days of deprivation." They were also reminders to me to be forever thankful for his freedom.

The purple pajamas had also served another useful purpose. Working with her dad at ADI brought Leslie into almost daily contact with the sons and daughters of the men who were still missing in Southeast Asia, and she felt a strong empathy with them. Now young adults like Leslie, these POW children were extremely vocal activists, and Leslie had participated in one of their public demonstrations. My heart had stood still as I watched her, long blond hair shining in the sun, wearing the striped pajamas Red had worn in the Hanoi Hilton, wrists bound with heavy chains to the wrists of the daughter of a missing man, walk single-file and silent down Pennsylvania Avenue to the White House.

"It could be my dad," she had explained to one of the reporters waiting in Lafayette Park.

The purple-striped prisoner's uniform had become a symbol for all of us, a reminder of how blessed we were to be together. It was when our family gathered at Christmas that Red was able to lay down the burden of trying to do something about the men who had not come home. I loved to see him so relaxed. But, even then, the occasional faraway look in his eyes told me he was thinking of men who were spending their fifteenth, or eighteenth, Christmas in POW camps in the jungles of Southeast Asia.

Dave noticed it, too. Dave had gotten to know his dad very well during the congressional campaign in 1982, and he had this to say about Red in 1989:

On May 19, 1967, my neatly structured and carefree seven-year-old world suddenly shattered. For the preceding eight months, my father had been fighting the war in Vietnam, but I had known where he was, and that he was coming home. In fact, he was sort of a folk hero for me and my friends.

Before he had left for Vietnam, there were times when my friends and I would be playing football in the back yard, and my mother would come out on the screened-in back porch and shout, "David, your father just called from Oceana. He's getting ready to take off and he's going to fly over the house." Sure enough, in a few minutes his A-6 Intruder jet would come streaking low over the back yard and he would tip his wings. Needless to say, this was pretty impressive to a group of seven-year-olds and I was very proud. So for the past eight months my father had been away fighting the Vietnam War in that big, fast jet that we had watched fly over the back yard. That gave me a little extra status among the kids whose fathers left home every morning at 9:00 and returned at 5:00 in the afternoon in the family station wagon.

On the day my father was shot down, I knew something very bad had happened in my happy little world. I came home from school to find the house full of strange people. Later, I went out to play and scratched myself in a briar patch. I came running home and saw that the people were all still there. As I went into the kitchen looking for my mother and the band-aids, I noticed that although the house was full of people, it was strangely quiet. It reminded me of church on Sunday, during a silent prayer.

"Mom," I cried when I found her, "I hurt myself."

"Go next door to Mrs. Mitchell's, David," my mom replied. "She'll give you a band-aid. Then come back and get your pajamas. You're spending the night with the Mitchells." As I walked outside, I knew that something was very wrong. I had come home with a scrape, and my mother had sent me to the neighbor's. And she wanted me to stay there all night.

The next morning, when I got home, my mother asked me to sit down on the porch steps beside her. She put her arms around me. Then she told me that my father's plane had been shot down over North Vietnam and that he had parachuted into the jungle. Later, when the Navy said he had probably been captured, I was sure that he was still hiding in the jungle. But as the weeks and then months passed, I started to give up hope that he would be rescued and, in my own way, I began to accept the fact that he might not come home at all. I remember wondering about what type of animals roamed the jungles of North Vietnam. I tried to visualize how the North Vietnamese soldiers looked, what kind of hats they wore, and things like that. But at my young age, I was able to push it out of my mind most of the time. Three years later, when Hanoi announced that he was alive and being held captive, I thought about him more and more.

As the years went by and I grew up, I thought more often about him and what he might be going through. Once in a while, I would lie on my back in the grass on a sunny day and stare at the sky. I couldn't shake the thought that somewhere thousands of miles away, I had a father that I hadn't seen or talked to for years, and that he might indeed be lying on his back somewhere, staring at the same blue sky. It was strange, but I felt that the sky was our only bond. It was the one thing that we could share.

Later, I began to have serious doubts about whether I would ever see him again. But I kept these doubts to myself because the rest of the family was always optimistic. At least outwardly they were.

In early 1973, when the Paris Peace Accords were signed, I was skeptical. I didn't want to get my hopes up that my father would return until I knew he was actually on his way home. When we knew that he was actually being released, I was apprehensive about what he would be like. I wondered how it would feel to have a father at the dinner table again. Naval experts warned us that he might return with severe physical or psychological problems. I wasn't quite sure what to expect, and I was very nervous, but in an excited sort of way. The moment I saw him walk down the ramp from the plane in the Philippines, I sensed that my fears were unnecessary. I had never been prouder or happier in my life. Once he returned to Virginia Beach and the media attention faded, our family returned to what was normal for other families in a remarkably short time. After two weeks back, it almost seemed as if he had never been gone. It was remarkable! I give my mother a lot of the credit for the smooth transition of his return because she had worked so hard over the years to make sure that we children were aware of what an integral part of our family our father was. But to this day, I am amazed at how rapidly and smoothly our family adjusted to being back together.

Getting to know my father, for what seemed like the first time, was fascinating. He lived up to every expectation I had accumulated over the years of separation. I found him to be a man with very strong convictions and the determination to stand behind those convictions with intense loyalty. His love of God, country, and family became obvious immediately. After hearing about the brutal and barbaric torture that he endured in captivity, I wondered how any human could withstand such treatment. I soon realized that my father has a keen competitive spirit that, along with his faith in God, pulled him through those darkest hours of suffering. That same love of competition surely accounted for all of the

sports trophies, clippings from sports pages, and athletic scholarships he accumulated through the years before becoming a Navy
pilot. When he returned from Vietnam, he couldn't wait to get
back up to speed as an aviator and continue with his naval career.
Although I'm sure his eagerness was mostly due to his strong
sense of duty to his country, I can't help but believe that part of
this eagerness came from his competitive desire to catch up with
his colleagues. In fact, when my father retired from the Navy and
decided to run for Congress as a conservative Republican in a
North Carolina congressional district that had elected only Democrats for the last hundred years, his competitive nature surfaced
again. I questioned him on the wisdom of running as a Republican in a district where there were nine registered Democrats to
every registered Republican.

"David," he said, "this country needs people to fight in Congress
for a strong national defense and the protection of our precious
freedom. And, besides, we're going to win despite the odds."

Well, we lost the election, but we mounted the only serious threat
that the Democratic party in that district has seen in this century.
Moreover, we reestablished the existence of a two-party system in
that part of North Carolina. That was crucial because of the in-
herent dangers of a one-party system of government. Out of that
effort in North Carolina and the tremendous outpouring of public support which resulted came the American Defense Foundation (ADF) and the American Defense Institute (ADI). Watching
ADF/ADI grow over the years has made me extremely proud of
my father. His sense of duty to his country and his steadfast determination to stand behind his beliefs has been a constant source of
inspiration to me. He had a vision for that organization and he
made it happen.

The main thing I have come to respect about my father as I've
grown to know him since his return from Vietnam is the value he
places on integrity. Many people I've come to know in my life who
possess a competitive nature pursue victory or success at the
expense of their integrity. They have the "succeed at any cost"
mentality. My father, on the other hand, maintains an uncompro-
mising integrity.

When I was in high school, we moved to Pensacola, Florida,
where my father assumed command of the aircraft carrier USS
Lexington. Many of the returned prisoners of war from Vietnam
came to the Naval Aviation Medical Center there for their annual
medical examinations, so I had the opportunity to meet and talk
with many of the men alongside whom my father spent his years

in captivity. Over and over, these men would tell me how proud they were to have served their country with my father because of his integrity and his intense dedication to his values. I've always believed that a man is judged most critically by his peers. I considered what these brave men who served with my father under some of the most barbaric conditions imaginable said about him to be the highest form of praise.

Now that my father has become involved in the fight to see that all U.S. servicemen who are still held captive in Southeast Asia are accounted for, there are those in our government who are seeking to discredit him. I cannot begin to understand why anyone in our government would attempt to attack the integrity of a man who spent six years in a communist prison in service to his country simply because he is seeking the return of his comrades who were left behind. But I do know one thing: they will never be able to tarnish the integrity of my father.

My father has given me the most important gift of all: the background to succeed as a person. There is no one that I know, have heard of, or read about, that I would be more proud to call my father than Red McDaniel.

David McDaniel, 1989

21

. . . And They Filled My Heart with Gladness

I was holding my breath.

Mike was home for a rare between-Christmases visit. He and Red had just come from the golf course, where Mike had beaten his dad at golf for the first time ever. They were standing in the kitchen.

"I want to help you, Dad," Mike was saying. "I like what you're doing and I think I can help."

I knew Red was looking for an executive director for ADI. The staff had kept things going without much-needed management, and it was time to bring in someone who could lead the rapidly growing organization into the months and years ahead.

Surely Red hasn't asked Mike to do it. He has his own life, a good job, a home in San Diego. This isn't his battle!

"You'd be great, Mike. I need somebody with your brains and your administrative ability, but I don't know. Would it be beneficial for you? Can you afford it? Salaries aren't very good. What about your career?" Red's eyes searched Mike's.

"I love my job, Dad. I have a good future there. But, you know, I want to do something that's going to really make a difference. Ship repair is important, yes. But how does it specifically affect the future? I think what you're doing is really exciting! I want to do it, if you want me. What do you think, Mom?"

I took a deep breath. *It would be wonderful*, I thought, *having him here, seeing Michael and Daryl grow up, being a part of their lives. But what about Mike and Deb? Will working at ADI jeopardize their future? What about Mike giving up his career, having to sell their home? What about Deb? Will she be happy here? It will be a very different lifestyle. Can Mike handle working with his dad every day?*

"I think you should be very selfish, Mike. Don't do it to help your dad. Do what's best for you and Deb and the boys," I said.

"All my life you've tried to teach me to think of other people and now you're telling me to be selfish?" Mike laughed.

I just looked at him. My little ten-year-old boy who had tried to hold his tears back when his dad was shot down, the little guy who had bought a bunch of daisies to "help Mom be happy" years ago, had grown into this six-foot-three-inch man, still eager to help.

"Well, Red, you're looking for staff people who'll be loyal to you and to ADI. Just think how loyal this one will be!" I said.

Mike grinned broadly.

"Well, I also want my kids to know their grandparents."

We laughed and cried and hugged each other, and Mike flew back to San Diego to talk it over with Deb. When he came home for Christmas that year, he had Deb, Michael, Daryl, the family dog Brandy, and all their possessions in tow. The day after New Year's, the American Defense Institute and the American Defense Foundation had an executive director, something we had needed from the very beginning.

One of the first letters Mike wrote as ADI's executive director was to Glen Urquhart, a prominent Washington businessman who had supported Red's effort to get the POWs home, and had offered the encouragement Red needed for what he had called the toughest battle of his life. In his letter to Glen, Mike wrote:

Dear Glen,

I wanted to express my appreciation for your financial support of the POW/MIA project. Most of all, I want to thank you for your moral support for my dad's efforts. It really means a lot to him, more than you may know.

I have watched my dad's battle for the POWs from the sidelines over the last few years. As you know, it is not a very popular cause with many people and much of the time my dad goes "against the grain." About a year ago, when I was out for a visit from San Diego, I said to him, "Look at all the flak you have to take. Why do you do it?" My dad responded, "Because it's the right thing to do." That's the trait I admire so much in my dad. That is the trait that I hope to exemplify some day.

Sincerely,

Mike McDaniel
Executive Director

I came across Mike's letter while I was helping with the filing in the ADI office. When I read what he had written, I knew my oldest son's life already exemplified the integrity of his dad.

No greater fortune can come to a man than to know the causes he gave his life to on this earth will continue after he leaves it—and that his own children are willing to take up his battles. That's what Mike's coming to ADI did for his dad.

And no greater fortune can come to a woman than to know her children heard what she tried to tell them all those years: true happiness is found in giving yourself to others. That's what Mike's coming to ADI did for me.

Mike, David, and Leslie had known great tragedy early in their lives. They grew up in a house filled with turmoil and pain. But they survived. Their pain filled them with compassion for the struggles of those around them. They learned about courage, and they learned about faith. I knew that they would not hesitate to take up the gauntlet, to fight for the causes they knew to be right.

They were my children and they filled my heart with gladness.

22

The Book and the Senators

I had hoped we would resolve the POW issue before Mike joined the staff at ADI, or at least reach a point where we could say we'd done all we could do to rectify what we saw as a terrible injustice to America's fighting men.

Red agreed with me. He didn't want to expose his son to the bombardment in Washington. In mid-1988, when it was decided that Mike would come to ADI "next January," they made big plans for expanding the organization "after the POWs are home."

"The POW issue will be resolved by the end of the year, Mike," Red had told him. "It has to be."

"What if it isn't, Dad?" Mike had asked. "I'm not afraid of it."

"It will be. But if it isn't, I'm going to hang it up then," Red had responded. "I can't think of anything else we can do."

He had been to everyone he knew who could help: members of Congress, high-level officials in the Reagan administration, people out of government who he knew had influence with the president and with the most powerful congressional leaders.

Most of the influential people he contacted couldn't believe the men were still alive. Those who thought it might be true were reluctant to get into something that might go deeper than they were willing to explore. They seemed to be afraid they'd find some secret buried deep in the bureaucracy that they wouldn't know how to handle. And one friend in the intelligence community gave Red a dire warning,

"It's a suicide mission you're on, ol' buddy. You're getting into the more sinister echelons of government now."

"What happened to government of the people and by the people?" Red wanted to know.

"We've gotten more sophisticated, Red—and more secretive," his friend replied. "Grow up! We've adopted "the ends justify the means" philosophy in government. In other words, if it works, do it. That's just the way it is, my friend. All your idealism isn't going to change it."

"Then what are all our wars about?" Red asked him. "Why fight, if our philosophy is the same as the enemy's? Seems to me there are some fundamental principles at risk here."

"You're hopeless, Red," was the reply. "Good luck. You're going to need it. You won't find many takers out there. People are deathly afraid of something like this."

Red refused to believe that things were as bad as his cynical friend in intelligence thought. He couldn't believe that there was really official approval of any "sinister echelon of government," although he had heard that secret operations could go awry without the proper oversight. And he was certain that he could find plenty of "takers"—people of courage who wouldn't be afraid to look at anything in the government that might be considered "sinister." He was sure the NAMPOW organization, made up of men who had been imprisoned with him in Vietnam, would rally to the cause of finding out what had happened to those who didn't return.

"They're men of courage," he told me. "They know how it feels to be a POW, to wonder when your country's going to come and get you. When we go to the NAMPOW reunion in Virginia Beach, I'm going to ask the guys to request a presidential commission to look into the evidence that Americans are still in captivity over there. They can't say no to that, can they?"

But NAMPOW turned him down. It was "too political," they told him, and NAMPOW was strictly a "fraternal" organization.

"He shouldn't bring this up," I heard a voice behind me at the meeting say. "This is a social gathering."

I turned around and saw that the voice belonged to a young wife who had met and married her husband after he came home.

I guess I can't blame her for not wanting Red to spoil the party, I thought. *She can't know how it feels to be a wife still waiting. But what about the others? They know. Where's the courage?*

Red was feeling pretty low when we left Virginia Beach.

"If they won't get involved, I don't know who will," he said. But some of the men who had been in the POW camps with Red had seen the evidence themselves, and they were fighting the battle as individuals in their own way. I had always considered Robbie Risner a man of great courage. Now I admired him even more, as he jumped into the fray with Red. Laird Gutterson, Larry Stark, John Parsels, Bill Baugh, and Terry Uyeyama* were also added to my list of courageous men, as they ignored the consequences and fought the battle for the POWs who were left behind. As time went by, others contacted Red and offered their help.

But most of the former POWs just didn't want to see the evidence. I tried to understand that. They'd fought their battles. They wanted to live out the rest of their lives in peace. I could understand that. But I couldn't understand their attitude toward Red. It almost seemed as though they were angry with him for his own involvement, for trying to get them involved. Some of them were openly hostile, and word got back to us about a comment one of them had made about Red.

A friend of Red's had seen a former POW at a party and said to this man casually, "I saw your friend Red McDaniel the other day."

"Red McDaniel's not *my* friend; he's not one of us," said the man who had been locked up with Red in the Hanoi Hilton.

I knew that had to hurt. But Red shrugged it off.

"He doesn't want to see it," Red said. "Because if he does, he'll have to start questioning the system that called him a hero. He knows how I performed in Hanoi, that I stack up with the rest of them. But he can't look at this issue. If he does, and he does nothing about it, he won't be able to look himself in the mirror every morning. And all of us need to be able to look in the mirror.

---

*After the book Monika and Bill were writing was published, many more of the former Vietnam POWs joined Red's battle for those who had not returned.

"I've been where he is," he continued. "Blind faith. My country can do no wrong. I used to believe that."

"So did Hitler's soldiers," I said thoughtfully. "Ask no questions. Just follow orders. You know, Red, I would think Ross Perot's involvement would be convincing to the men who were in the Hanoi Hilton. They know how much he did for all of you guys during the war. And they have great respect for him."

Red had helped me understand why the POWs refused to look at the evidence, but I had a hard time understanding why so few politicians were willing to get involved.

"We're finding out what they're really made of, Dorothy."

Red was talking about politicians he had come to admire as men who would stand up for their convictions on the issues. But most of them seemed to want to bury their heads on this one. It just wasn't good politics to be concerned about a handful of men who went away years ago to a war most people wanted to forget. And these men who wanted to ignore the issue were the ones who *could* do something.

A few of them stepped out to the battle line. Congressmen Bob Smith of New Hampshire and John Rowland of Connecticut led the POW activists in Congress. They were the ones who provided the counterattack when letters from other congressmen and the Defense Intelligence Agency attempting to discredit Red and ADI were circulated on Capitol Hill.

Thirty-five other senators and congressmen agreed to help raise the money for the reward we'd offered for the safe return of a POW. Congressmen Hank Brown of Colorado and Dave Dreier of California both drafted amendments which would focus attention on the abandoned men. But for the most part, it was business as usual in Congress. And Red knew the POWs were running out of time.

Members of Congress came regularly to ADI for information on many defense issues, and they were beginning to come to ADI for information on the POW issue. People in their districts were becoming more aware of what they saw as a national disgrace: the abandonment of American servicemen after a battle. We were called on to supply a great deal of information for congressional offices to provide to their constituents, but there were very few meaningful initiatives taken by the congressmen themselves.

Then Senator Jesse Helms offered an amendment which would give the American people a chance to donate a dollar to the POW reward by checking a box on their individual income tax returns. The Helms Amendment started a firestorm on Capitol Hill, and eventually led to a full-fledged Senate investigation. Senator Helms was joined by Senator Charles Grassley, and they spent long months looking into the federal government's handling of POW evidence.*

A 1986 Pentagon panel, chaired by the former Director of the Defense Intelligence Agency, General Eugene Tighe, had concluded that as many as 100 Americans were still held prisoner in Southeast Asia. The Senate investigators wanted to find out, among other things, why the Tighe Report had immediately been classified, thereby preventing any of the panel members from divulging its contents to the public.

Red was greatly encouraged when these two powerful senators began to look into the POW issue. (After the 1990 elections, Helms and Grassley were joined by three allies. POW champions in the House of Representatives, Congressmen Bob Smith, Hank Brown, and Larry Craig, were elected to the Senate.) Red shared all the information he had accumulated through the years with the staff members conducting the investigation. When they began their investigation, the staff members for the two senators requested a briefing by the Defense Intelligence Agency. At the briefing, the investigators told Red, an Army colonel had warned them to stop asking questions or "the same thing will happen to your bosses that has happened to other members of Congress." We had wondered why some congressmen had seemed to suddenly lose interest, and now we wondered if there had been some sort of intimidation of these elected officials. This was a scary thought, in a democratic government.

Now the battle was not such a lonely one, but progress was agonizingly slow. Red had high hopes that the Senate investigation

---

*The Senate investigators issued an interim report on Oct. 29, 1990, which received wide press coverage and vindicated the POW activists' claim that the Defense Intelligence Agency had disregarded proof of living Americans in Southeast Asia (see appendix B). At this writing, the Senate investigation is ongoing.

would eventually resolve the POW issue, but he was impatient. He knew that every passing day was a matter of life or death for the POWs, and he wondered aloud how many men had died since he first started asking questions on their behalf in 1985.

Red knew there was only so much he could do himself. He decided that the publication of the book he was working on with Monika Jensen and Bill Stevenson would be his final effort. For two years he had supplied material and contacts for the writing of *Kiss the Boys Goodbye: How the United States Betrayed Its Own POWs in Vietnam.** Monika, a former "60 Minutes" producer, and Bill, a reknowned intelligence expert and best-selling author, would research the POW story in greater depth than had been done so far. Their findings were explosive. Red saw the book as the best way to get the POW story before the American people, and he put Monika and Bill in touch with every source of information he knew. One source led to another, and the authors soon developed a network of people all over the world who were troubled by the covert activities being carried out in America's name, activities that Monika and Bill found had kept American POWs in their cells for more than a decade after the end of the war. These knowledgable sources were willing to risk talking about it, now that someone was willing to write about it.

Monika and Bill came down from their home in Toronto often during those two years to stay with us while they pored over Red's POW files and listened to the tapes we had started making in 1985. When the manuscript was complete and ready to go to the publisher, Bill called Red.

"We want you and Dorothy to come to Toronto to read the manuscript," he said. "We don't want to risk sending it through the mails. From what we've learned about the opposition, they'll do anything they can to keep this story from being told!"

So Red and I flew to Toronto for a weekend and took turns reading the one copy of the manuscript for two days and nights. To see the entire story on paper was a sobering experience for both

---

Kiss the Boys Goodbye, published in Canada by McClelland and Stewart and in the U.S. by E.P. Dutton, was released in September 1990. The book has also been published in Great Britain.

of us. Some of the information Bill and Monika had uncovered even Red hadn't known, and, for the first time, all the myriad pieces of the giant puzzle fit together coherently.

"It's a masterpiece!" Red told Monika as she drove us back to the airport on Sunday night. "If this book doesn't do it, nothing will. The American people will be up in arms when *Kiss the Boys Goodbye* hits the bookstores. When will that be?"

"Don't hold your breath, Red," Monika answered grimly. "We have to get it published first. The contract is firm, but don't underestimate your enemy. Anything can happen, you know.

"By the way, we're putting your name on the title page. 'With Material from Captain Eugene "Red" McDaniel (United States Navy, Retired),' it says. We couldn't have done it without your help."

"Well, you were able to take all the information Red has gathered and put it together so people can understand what is a very complicated issue," I volunteered. "Even *I* have trouble with it, and I hear it all day, every day."

Red grinned, triumphant.

"That's going to change now, Dorothy," he said. "This is it. I've done all I can. Now it's up to the American people."

I could only hope he meant it.

Red had known from the beginning that he himself could not bring the POWs home, not even with the help of those who agreed with him. He knew to bring them home would require a high-level decision to negotiate seriously for their release, a willingness by people more powerful than he to uncover bureaucratic crimes and let the chips fall wherever they would. The American people would have to demand the men's return and they *would*; he was sure they would, after they read *Kiss the Boys Goodbye* and learned about the findings of the ongoing Senate investigation.

Some of the POW activists, especially those who were Vietnam veterans, wanted to go on Rambo-like missions, to make illegal forays across the borders of the communist countries where the men were held, raid the camps, and rescue the POWs. Red suspected that some of them had tried. But he tried to discourage the would-be Rambos from taking matters into their own hands. It was dangerous and illegal and *could* result in even more Americans in enemy hands. And he didn't see how such raids could possibly be successful in bringing out any POWs.

Then, too, he didn't want to give up his belief that the system would work, that the people could force the politicians to act. So he had continued doggedly, in the face of fierce opposition, to get the story of the abandoned men out before the public, on the front pages of the newspapers, and into the halls of power.

Now he could put all that behind him and get on with the task of expanding the American Defense Institute, adding new defense priorities to the agenda and developing new programs to prepare young Americans to lead the nation in the twenty-first century.

He felt certain that the continuing battle for the POWs would have a far-reaching impact on national policy, affecting the conduct of future wars and future decisions concerning missing U.S. servicemen and women. After he read the manuscript of *Kiss the Boys Goodbye* and learned of some of the more unsavory activities that Monika and Bill had uncovered, he hoped the battle for the POWs would also demonstrate the need for more careful oversight of America's covert activities throughout the world. The battle would surely restore one of the nation's most fundamental principles: each individual counts; each person has value. He had made it *his* battle, and he had given it everything he had.

23

God Sees the Scars

Lindsey Powell was speaking from the pulpit in our church in Alexandria. A young Air Force officer who had studied for the ministry before he joined the Air Force, Lindsey was delivering the sermon while the pastor was away.

"Throughout history, there has always been wickedness in high places," he said.

From the corner of my eye I saw Red lean forward, muscles straining under his gray flannel jacket. Jaw taut, he was listening intently as Lindsey described some biblical examples of "wickedness in high places."

I had prayed that Red's disillusionment with the high-ranking officials responsible for the abandonment of the POWs wouldn't do him in, leaving him bitter and despairing. The Vietnamese Communists had not been able to break his spirit. The ultimate tragedy would be for his own countrymen to do what his enemy in Vietnam could not.

"You and I are called to fight injustice and unethical conduct in high places. We do it simply because it is right. We leave the results to God.

"'The eyes of God move to and fro across the whole earth seeking a man whose heart is perfect toward Him,'" Lindsey read from the Scriptures.

Then he said, "When the eyes of God examine a man's heart,

they look for his scars, the scars from his battles for justice and righteousness."*

I glanced at Red again. I thought back to the long and lonely days the children and I had waited for him to return. My own battle had been against self-pity, disillusionment, and despair. Sooner or later, I knew, those who inflict pain and injustice receive their just reward. It was that belief that had held me back from bitterness.

Red had finally reached the point where he could walk away from the battle for the POWs, knowing that he had done his best. He had learned a hard lesson. His beloved country was capable of, was in fact guilty of, betrayal of some of her finest and bravest soldiers. I hoped he could live with that knowledge in some kind of peace.

Finally we could let the battle scars heal and get on with what we really wanted to do: build our organization, play with our grandchildren, maybe even take some time off, now that Mike was running ADF and ADI. Mike was the best thing that had happened to ADF and ADI since we started the organizations in 1983. He had the energy and the administrative ability to help ADF and ADI thrive, and he was already making long-range plans for future growth, expanding the existing programs for young people and establishing several new ones. One new program, Pride in America, was an ambitious project which would go into the nation's high schools to develop a sense of community and national pride among the young people Mike called "our future leaders."

I had a feeling that Mike would never give up on the POWs. While Red was becoming more and more disillusioned, Mike was becoming more and more angry about the abandonment of American servicemen.

"How can we go into high schools to ask young people to care about their country when we know their country won't care about them if they are ever captured by the enemy in time of war?" he asked Red. "And what about Michael and Daryl? I'm thinking about them, too, and about all my friends from the Naval Acad-

*The idea for Lindsey Powell's sermon came from page 18, *Broadman Comments* 1988–89, published by Broadman Press, Nashville, TN.

emy who'll be the ones who fly the missions if we go to war in the Middle East or somewhere else."

He was spending long hours with the Senate investigators, and he had learned that leaving men behind was a policy pattern. It had happened in Korea and also in World War II, he said, and it would surely happen again if the Senate investigations were not successful in changing the policy toward America's missing men.

He knew, too, that nothing would come of the Senate report and *Kiss the Boys Goodbye* if they weren't publicized, and he wanted ADI to take on the task of informing the American people about the book and the Senate report. He understood the power of the grassroots both from my fight to bring his dad home and from his own "Don't Let Them Be Forgotten" campaigns as a twelve-year-old.

My heart skipped a beat when Mike mentioned his friends from the Naval Academy, who were now full-fledged naval aviators. I knew them well; they had spent many days in our home in Alexandria while they were midshipmen, and they were like my own sons. Mike himself would no doubt be called back to active duty in the event of war.

"We're not going to war in the Middle East," I protested. "We aren't, are we? Would they have to call up the reserves if we did?"

"Of course they would, Mom. That's what the reserves are for. And, yes, we could have a war in the Middle East, and if we did I would *want* to do my part!"

It was coming closer to home again. I knew I couldn't bear to see another person I loved go into combat. Maybe we wouldn't be able to let the battle scars heal after all.

Even though I still wasn't convinced that the book Red had helped Monika and Bill write and the continuing Senate investigation would bring the men home, I felt sure that we had accomplished a great deal. Surely our work had changed the picture for any future POWs and for their families. In the next war, the one B.R. and Red had said was almost inevitable, I hoped that POW/MIA families wouldn't have to beat the streets for support the way Vietnam POW/MIA family members had had to do. The flyers who found themselves floating down over enemy territory after high-speed ejections would know that their country would not abandon them to fate, and knowing that would surely give them the strength to endure. Congressmen would know about the Geneva Conventions and whether or not the enemy was signatory to the international agreements regarding the treatment of prisoners of war.

Some of the men who had gone down over Southeast Asia weren't going to make it, I knew. It had been so long; some of them, no doubt, had already given up and died. How did it feel, I wondered, to spend your last minutes in a POW cell wondering why your country didn't come to get you?

"I could have lasted a lot longer, Dorothy," Red said. "You'd be surprised how much a man can take, with God's help. The flak I've taken since I got into this battle here for the POWs is much worse than the torture and isolation I endured in the Hanoi Hilton. The toughest part for the men now is knowing they've been abandoned."

I knew that Red had decided a year ago that he had done all he could, that his work with the writing of *Kiss the Boys Goodbye* and with the Senate investigators would be his final effort. But then an American attorney who practiced law in Paris called Red.

"I understand you've offered a reward for an American POW. I have a taker. He says he can bring eight out right away. And there'll be more, if you handle this first release well."

At first Red was skeptical. There had been other such calls, earlier, when the reward was first publicized.

"We've tried to give our information to the U.S. embassy here and to a prominent senator," the attorney continued. "Nobody's interested."

"You know we have to check this out; it could be for real," Red said to Mike and me.

After a series of transatlantic phone calls and face-to-face meetings with the attorney and the Vietnamese who said they could deliver the eight Americans, Red was convinced this was the break he had been seeking since 1985.

He was so excited.

"This is it! But we have to hurry. Someone, somewhere, does not want these men to come home. I don't know who it is. And I don't know whether or not they can stop it. I do know our government is getting ready to establish diplomatic relations with Hanoi. This may be our last chance to make a deal for the POWs," he continued.

The unseen enemy again, I thought. *Why would anyone not want POWs to come home?*

There were numerous contacts with the Vietnamese living in Paris as the months wore on. And then there was silence.

"It's like watching grass grow," Red said. "Maybe we should just give it up. The Vietnamese told me that one of the Americans has died since we started talking to them."

So he tried to put it on hold once again, to continue his other defense projects, perhaps to give it up altogether this time.

"Red, you've done all you can," I said. And I thought he agreed with me.

A trip to Fort Bragg, North Carolina, convinced him he couldn't give up on the POWs. He spoke to the troops about voting and he told them how valuable their service to the nation was to the preservation of freedom. He didn't mention the POW effort.

But the troops did.

After Red finished speaking, he was approached by two members of Delta, the elite Special Forces group which carries out top-secret missions all over the world.

"I want to thank you for what you are doing for the men we left behind in Southeast Asia," one of them said. "I have come to the conclusion that someone in our government doesn't want those men to come home. In the past eighteen months, we have planned two different rescue missions into Southeast Asia. We knew where the men were. We knew how many men were there. We were ready to go. We were excited about it. But, at the last minute, both times, someone cancelled the mission.

"Captain, those men have been abandoned by this country. There're no two ways about it. Thank God for men like you who refuse to let that happen."

The other soldier had listened intently. Now he spoke, brown eyes flashing.

"Captain," he asked. "Have you thought about organizing a private rescue mission? If you ever do, I can get a group of guys together to go in there and get our men out."

Red explained to the two soldiers that he couldn't condone any kind of illegal incursion to rescue POWs.

"Well, if you change your mind, just let us know," the first soldier spoke again. "If you need twenty men, give me a week. If you need fifty men, it will take a little longer. At Delta, we don't believe in leaving men behind."

The full impact of the soldier's words didn't sink in until Red was aboard the plane to Washington.

"We don't believe in leaving men behind."

Neither do the American people, Red said to himself. The American people just take for granted that their government will meet its end of the bargain with our fighting men. And if the government doesn't keep that commitment, it violates one of the principles that made America. America can have the biggest defense budget in history and the most powerful military arsenal that can be built, but we'll lose the battle if we lose our integrity.

What had begun for Red as a question about the fate of his navigator and a handful of forgotten POWs had grown into a question about the erosion of his country's fundamental values. And his search for ways to protect his country had become a battle to make sure his country was worth protecting. He had come to realize that America's strength lay in the keeping of her commitments and that, if integrity vanished from defense calculations, all the technology in the world would make no difference in the fight for freedom.

America's people knew that was true. They had rallied to his defense when he was held in a foreign land. His communist captors hadn't understood why the American people would be so concerned about such a small number of men in POW cells. He had wanted to say to them,

The American people would be concerned if there was only one man!

And the ordinary people he met every day, as he travelled around the country talking about patriotism and freedom, still held fast to the principles he had held onto, principles that had brought him through the ordeal of communist captivity.

By the time the plane touched down at National Airport, he knew that he would continue to fight freedom's battles, no matter what it cost him.

It was almost midnight when he got home.

He took off his shoes and socks and lay down on the bed beside me.

"Dorothy, we have to keep trying to solve the riddle of the POWs. For the men in Delta, for all the others who still serve, who want to believe in their country, we have to keep trying. For Mike, and his friends on active duty. For Michael and Daryl and Christopher and all the other grandchildren, we have to keep trying. I'm not sure we can ever get any of the men out of their cells and cages in Southeast Asia.

"But we have to keep trying to tell people about them. We have to make sure it never happens again."

I knew he was right. He had to keep trying, for the Delta troops and all the others. I knew he had to keep trying, for the young people who would serve in the future. And for the ordinary people, the ones who still believed in honor and integrity.

I looked at his ankles, white against the dark blue bedspread. The ugly purple scars from the leg irons he had worn in the Hanoi Hilton were still visible.

He reached up to turn off the lamp, fingers fumbling, still numb from the ropes that had bound his wrists so tightly.

I knew he would continue to fight. No doubt he would bear more scars. But he would bear them willingly, for the sake of his beloved country.

"God sees the scars," I whispered to the darkness.

Afterword

The publisher's galleys for *After the Hero's Welcome* arrived the day Lieutenant Zaun was shot down over Iraq. He was flying an A-6E Intruder from VA-35, Red's squadron. I saw Lieutenant Zaun's bruised and battered face and heard his halting words in front of Baghdad's TV cameras.

It's happening again! I cried. *It's starting all over again!*

Lieutenant Zaun's first name is Jeffrey, although it really isn't necessary to say that. All of America knows the name of the young Navy flyer who was paraded on TV after being tortured to say the words Saddam Hussein wanted him to say. To me, Jeffrey Zaun represents all the flyers who'll fly the missions over Iraq and end up in Saddam's POW camps. My heart reaches out to their families, casualties also of this new war, and I long to offer them encouragement and support.

It's happening again, but this time it's different.

The president of the United States is talking about the Geneva Conventions, reminding the world that Iraq is signatory to the international accords that mandate humane treatment of prisoners of war. So are the prime minister of Great Britain and the leaders of other civilized nations, and so are the American people. Red and other Vietnam POWs are being deluged by calls from TV and radio stations, newspapers and magazines from all over the nation. The news media know how much the people care about

America's sons who fall into the hands of the enemy. The Vietnam POWs are men who were incarcerated for six, seven, eight, and in one case *nine* years, and they survived their ordeal. They talk about torture and pain. They also talk about strength, and they talk about the faith that sustained them. The experiences Red and the other POWs had in the Hanoi Hilton have been incorporated into the training that will enable Lieutenant Zaun to survive his captivity. He will survive, and he will come home when the war in the Persian Gulf is over.

"This won't be another Vietnam." The president has given us his pledge. This time, American troops won't fight with their hands tied behind their backs. Lieutenant Zaun and the other POWs in Iraq won't have to sacrifice years of their lives to a lost cause. The Gulf War will not be a protracted war, and the members of our armed forces will not have to apologize for their service in it.

I hope these differences are comforting to the families of Jeffrey Zaun and other American POWs in the Middle East. They are to me. This time, America's missing men will not be forgotten, and none of them will be abandoned.

"He that dwelleth in the secret place of the Most High shall abide under the shadow of the Almighty."

Every day I pray for Lieutenant Zaun and the others, in the now-certain knowledge that the shadow of the Almighty extends to Baghdad, just as it did to Hanoi.

* * *

The manuscript for *After the Hero's Welcome* was completed in November 1990. Its writing was my effort to tell of Red's and my experiences and to focus attention on the POWs who have not yet returned from Southeast Asia.

My first reaction to my publisher's suggestion that the book summarize what my experiences taught me about life and how to live it was apprehension. Who am I to give "how to cope" advice to people who find themselves in situations not of their choosing? My publisher pointed out that I had lived the role of service wife, single parent, POW wife, activist, candidate's wife, activist (again!)—none of these roles my own choice. "Surely from all that you can have something to share."

It is with a deep sense of humility that I offer the following:

First, I have learned that life is made up of *decisions*. "Don't base your life on your feelings," my father said to me. Decide to love when you don't. Decide to act when you can't. Choose a course of action, not for reasons of expedience or convenience, but, as Red said about his stand in the battle for the POWs, because it is *the right thing to do*.

I asked my friend Angela to read my manuscript and offer questions a reader might have. "I don't understand how you can not base your life on your feelings," she protested after reading it. I explained that, moody person that I am, I don't want to choose a course of action on something important based on whether I have a headache that day, or didn't get enough sleep the night before. My decision to defy the keep-silent rule and focus public attention on Red and our family was carefully considered; had I jumped into the spotlight too soon, when my heart ruled my head, it probably would have been a disaster. I assured Angela, and I assure others who read my story, that the right feelings will follow the right decisions.

My answer to Angela leads me to my second lesson: I must care deeply about my cause. The one ingredient that enabled a handful of POW wives and mothers to get 200 million Americans, give or take a few, talking about our husbands and sons was our *passion*. When the Virginia Press Women awarded the POW wives their "Newsmakers of the Year" award in 1970, the citation read, in part, *"Armed with love, they are fighting the battle for their husbands..."* We loved our men, and we knew we'd never see them again if we *didn't* fight this battle.

Red has been able to make a small dent in a solid bureaucratic wall with his battle for the remaining men because of his *passion* for his cause. Now that the whole story has surfaced in *Kiss the Boys Goodbye* and the Senate investigation is in full swing, I believe those responsible for the betrayal of our POWs will finally be held accountable, and our nation will at last be purged of that awful crime. Our nation will be stronger and better because the people finally saw a wrong and decided to make it right. Already there is an outpouring of concern and outrage from people who've read *Kiss the Boys Goodbye*. Press interest in the issue is building, partly as a result of the efforts being made by Mike and the ADI staff. Both Red and Mike are working to publicize the book and the reports of the ongoing Senate investigation as they are released. Now that America is at war in the Middle East, there's an urgency to resolving the fate of the men America left behind in Southeast Asia. I pray that some of them will be returned before the United States completes plans to normalize relations with Vietnam. It may be too late for some of the abandoned men by the time any meaningful action is taken on their behalf, but perhaps such a tragedy will never be allowed to happen again, because Red and a few, a very few, others cared deeply.

Would-be activists must first measure the depth of their own commitment. How much do I care? I know that caring is contagious; I have a trunkful of letters from people who wore the POW bracelets bearing Red's name to prove it. The letters testify to the basic goodness of the American people. The politicians underestimate grassroots America. But I know that an individual can turn on the American people with his or her own passion, and that a minority of one can start a "movement" any day of the week. The capacity of our people for caring is unlimited; the secret is the activist's own commitment.

But the movement started by one will fizzle out and die if the "founder" doesn't persevere. Our wonderful, caring people have short memories. In America, we're accustomed to instant everything; we want things to happen *now*. And when they don't, we forget about them. Once an issue is on the front page, it must stay there. That's the hard part, but it can be done, if we care enough. We do care enough about the men in Southeast Asia and about those who are fighting the battles in the Middle East. So we will continue to work to keep them on the front pages of America's newspapers.

I consider myself very fortunate to have learned the third lesson early. It's a lesson that is hard to put into words, although many have tried. "Accentuate the positive," the songwriter suggested. "Look on the bright side," someone offered as his own homespun philosophy. The Bible says, "Trouble produces endurance" (among other things). I learned to look for the "up" side of every "down" side. As a military wife, I realized that the love and appreciation Red and I had for one another was partly a result of the dreaded separations. We never took each other for granted, the way we might have done if he'd had a regular nine-to-five job. As my children grew up, I saw how the pain in their lives had built strength, love for one another, and compassion for others. I don't always see it during the storm, but I've been able to see the bright side often enough to be convinced that it is always there. I *will* see it eventually if I look hard enough. And, to me, it's almost always worth the pain to experience the joy, worth the battle to know the victory.

I hasten to add that underlying all the life principles I've learned is faith, that God-given ability to trust in "things not seen," to know that I can give my best effort and leave the results to God. I've learned that I can pray and He will hear me, that He will help me to decide when to accept the situation I am in and when to try to change it. I choose my battles carefully, knowing that when I stand for what is right, He stands with me. He sees the scars, and that's enough for me.

A

White House Memoranda

April 26, 1971

MEMORANDUM FOR: GENERAL HUGHES

FROM: H. R. HALDEMAN

With the demonstrations gaining ground after the Veterans' effort last week, we've got to be doubly sure we are keeping the POW wives in line. Is there anything you can think of that should be done at this point?

cc: Chuck Colson

THE WHITE HOUSE
Washington

April 29, 1971

MEMORANDUM FOR H. R. HALDEMAN

Subject: POW/MIA Wives

This is in response to your memorandum of April 26th on this subject.

You are aware of my increasing concern about purely PR therapy being effective for much longer. Nevertheless, after a meeting with Al Haig and Chuck Colson, I feel that increased efforts in the "cosmetic" area are warranted and indeed essential to keep the families with us during the critical period of the next six to eight weeks. In addition to personal daily contact with the National League of Families in a continuing effort to show our concern by attempting to keep them informed and solve problems for them, here are some of the other activities we plan.

Today, Ambassador Bruce will propose a package deal on the POW/MIA in Paris. This is a new concept which wraps up inpartial inspection, release of the sick and wounded and those imprisoned the longest, and internment in a neutral country. The President will be prepared to highlight this tonight at the Press Conference which should give it an even greater significance.

Henry Kissinger will have a meeting with the Board of Directors of the National League of Families on Saturday, 8 May.

The Vice President will address the National Red Cross Convention in Washington on 17 May on the POW/MIA issue (it may be that the President should reconsider and pre-empt him and I am making a separate proposal along those lines).

We are working to get Major Rowe (Army escapee from the Viet Cong) and Mrs. Joan Vinson, the National Coordinator for the National League of Families, on the David Frost Show to counter the extremely bad job done by Jane Fonda on this show.

General Chappie James appeared on the Today Show on 28 April and did a superb job of upholding the Administration's position and setting the POW/MIA matter in proper prospective.

Secretary Laird announced at a Washington luncheon in his honor, that neutral shipping was available and ready to repatriate prisoners or to intern them in a third country.

According to Al Haig, the next eight weeks are critical and the efforts of the Ad Hoc Coordinating Group on POW/MIA matters will be devoted to keeping the families on the reservation in order to buy this time.

BRIGADIER GENERAL JAMES D. HUGHES

MEMORANDUM

NATIONAL SECURITY COUNCIL

LIMITED OFFICIAL USE

INFORMATION

March 12, 1979

MEMORANDUM FOR: DAVID AARON

FROM: MICHEL OKSENBERG

SUBJECT: National League of Families Meeting with the President

Your response to my memorandum of March 7 asks why State cannot pursue the issue of the American defector.

State has pursued this issue, and the defector is now on his way home.

The point is that his return will generate new stories about the MIA issue and particularly about the possibility that additional Americans remain in Hanoi.

My own view is that it would be politically wise for the President to indicate his own continued concern with the MIAs.

This is a "right wing" issue, and I think it gains the President some politically to indicate his continued interest in the issue—particularly since he may be moving on the Vietnam front in the months ahead and since the Administration had implied earlier that it believed Vietnamese assurances that there were no live Americans left in Hanoi.

LIMITED OFFICIAL USE

MEMORANDUM

NATIONAL SECURITY COUNCIL

ACTION

October 30, 1979

MEMORANDUM FOR: ZBIGNIEW BRZEZINSKI

FROM: MICHEL OKSENBERG

SUBJECT: October 26 Letter from the National League of Families of American Prisoners and MIAs in Southeast Asia and My October 26 Meeting with Same Organization

You have received another letter from the National League of Families (Tab C). I also had a meeting with representatives of the League on Friday, October 26, a summary of which is at Tab B. In that meeting, the League leadership stated that Vietnamese refugees continue to report sightings of live Americans in Vietnam and that the League is increasingly convinced Vietnam holds live American MIAs.

I have drafted an appropriate reply at Tab A. As 1980 approaches, we must redouble our efforts to maintain close liaison with such organizations.

RECOMMENDATION:

That you sign the letter at Tab A to the National League.

That you briefly and orally inform the President of the League's view summarized above.

MEMORANDUM

NATIONAL SECURITY COUNCIL

ACTION

January 21, 1980

MEMORANDUM FOR: ZBIGNIEW BRZEZINSKI

FROM: MICHEL OKSENBERG

SUBJECT: Renewed League of MIA Families Request for Appointment

Once again, the National League of Families of American Prisoners and Missing in Southeast Asia seeks to meet you (Tab B).

They have nothing new to say, and I am capable of summarizing any developments for you. So I recommend turning down the request, and I will call Ann Griffiths separately to say you have instructed me to see her.

However, a letter from you is important to indicate that you take recent refugee reports of sighting of live Americans "seriously." This is simply good politics; DIA and State are playing this game, and you should not be the whistle blower. The idea is to say that the President is determined to pursue any lead concerning possible live MIAs.

Do not offer an opinion as to whether these leads are realistic. Apparently you revealed skepticism to Congressman Gilman, and my recommended letter to the League walks you back from that.

RECOMMENDATION:

That you sign the letter at Tab A to Ann Griffiths.

THE WHITE HOUSE
Washington

ACTION

MEMORANDUM FOR: THE PRESIDENT

FROM: ZBIGNIEW BRZEZINSKI

SUBJECT: Letter from National League of Families, April 18, 1979

The National League of Families remains convinced that live American POWs remain in Vietnam. They also believe you are not being adequately informed and that the bureaucracy is not pursuing the matter aggressively. They remain opposed to the renewal of case reviews which commenced last year.

I attach a letter from them to you (Tab B). This case has little merit, but the group must be treated in the compassionate manner they deserve.

I will answer them myself (Tab A), but wish to be able to say you saw their letter and asked me to reply.

RECOMMENDATION:

That you approve my letter to the League of Families at Tab A.

Approve _____   Disapprove _____

B

Interim Report on the Southeast Asian POW/MIA Issue

By the U.S. Senate Committee on Foreign Relations Republican Staff

Monday, October 29, 1990

Introduction

One year ago, the Ranking Minority Member of the Senate Committee on Foreign Relations assigned members of the Minority Staff to investigate the following three questions:

1.) Whether the United States Government has received and still possesses valid information concerning living prisoners of war missing in action—POW/MIAs—in Southeast Asia;

2.) Whether the U.S. Government has failed to act on such information; and,

3.) Whether the U.S. Government has acted improperly to intimidate and discredit sources of such information.

The primary purpose of this investigation has been, and will continue to be, to determine whether the U.S. government has handled the question in a truthful and effective manner. But if it results in a determination that even one POW may still be alive, it will result in a dividend of blessings.

The inquiry remains on-going. It is based not only on the review of thousands of classified and non-classified documents, but also upon hundreds of telephonic and face-to-face interviews with government officials and those affected by their decisions with regard to POW/MIAs. A full report will require much additional investigation and analysis. The following, however, represents an interim report at the conclusion of one year's work. It allows the presentation of some preliminary conclusions.

Preliminary Conclusions

The U.S. Government states it has no evidence that POWs were left behind in Southeast Asia. The official policy asserts that it is open to investigation of all reports. For example, the official Department of Defense (DOD) *POW/MIA Fact Book*, issued July, 1990, states:

Although we have thus far been unable to prove that Americans are still detained against their will, the information available to us precludes ruling out that possibility. Actions to investigate live sighting reports receive and will continue to receive necessary priority and resources based on the assumption that at least some Americans are still held captive. Should any report prove true, we will take appropriate action to ensure the return of those involved.

Notwithstanding this professed openness to new evidence, the U.S. Government has insisted since April 12, 1973, that it has no evidence of living POWs. In fact, on that date—at the conclusion of OPERATION HOMECOMING, which brought home 591 POWs—Dr. Roger Shields, then Assistant Secretary of Defense, stated that the DOD had "no evidence that there were any more POWs still alive in all of Indochina."

This assertion has been consistent. For example, last July, Col. Joseph A. Schlatter, then chief of the Defense Intelligence Agency's Special Office for POW/MIAs, was saying that "If we look at everything we collected during the war and everything we've collected since the war, we don't find any evidence that Americans are captive."

Furthermore, as late as October, 1990, an unnamed "senior State Department official" was quoted in the press as saying the U.S. Government has "no evidence" of living American prisoners in Southeast Asia.

However, to say that the U.S. Government has "no evidence" is not the same as saying that no evidence exists. After all, there have been nearly 11,700 reports relating to POW/MIAs over the years, including 1,400 first-hand, live-sighting reports. The question is whether every single one of these reports can be dismissed from the category of credible evidence.

The U.S. Government position makes sense only if every single one of these reports can be shown to have been fabricated, erroneous, or not relating directly to a POW/MIA—for example, some reports may relate to Europeans in the area. In fact, DIA analysts have rejected the evidence of all these reports, except for a small pool of less than 150 still considered "unresolved."

The preliminary conclusions presented by staff for review by Senators are as follows:

1. After the conclusion of OPERATION HOMECOMING in April, 1973, brought the return of the 591 POWs, official U.S.

Government policy internally adopted and acted upon the presumption that all other POWs were dead, despite public assertions that the government was still open to investigating the possibility of discovering the existence of living prisoners.

2. Following the adoption of an internal policy in April, 1973, that all POW/MIAs were presumed dead, the U.S. Government, convened commissions in each military service to consider each case on the POW/MIA list in order to make a statutory declaration of presumption of death.

3. While there is no reason to believe that the majority, if not most, of the declarations of presumptive death are incorrect, staff review of live-sighting report files at DIA found a disturbing pattern of arbitrary rejection of evidence that connected a sighting to a specific POW/MIA or U.S. POW/MIAs in general.

4. The pattern of arbitrary rejection resulted in a declaration of presumptive finding of death for every such individual case, except one.

5. The internal policy that all POW/MIAs were presumed dead resulted in an emphasis on finding and identifying remains of dead personnel, rather than searching for living POW/MIAs.

6. The desire to identify specific sets of remains with specific names on the POW/MIA list led DOD to an exaggeration of the capabilities of forensic science, and identification based on dubious presumptions and illogical deductions rather than actual physical identification—a process which resulted in numerous misidentifications of remains.

7. Despite adherence to internal policies and public statements after April, 1973 that "no evidence" existed of living POWs, DIA authoritatively concluded as late as April, 1974 that several hundred living POW/MIAs were still held captive in South East Asia.

8. Although the Pathet Lao declared on April 3, 1973, that Laotian Communist forces were holding American POWs and were prepared to give an accounting, nine days later a DOD spokesman declared that there were no more American prisoners anywhere in South East Asia. No POWs held by Laotian Communist forces ever returned. The evidence indicates that the U.S. Government made a decision to abandon U.S. citizens still in the custody

of the Socialist Republic of Vietnam, Laos and Cambodia, at the conclusion of U.S. involvement in the Second Indochina War.

9. U.S. casualties, including POW/MIAs in South East Asia, resulting from covert or cross border operation, may not be included on the list of those missing.

10. The executive branch has failed to address adequately the concerns of the family members of the POW/MIAs, and has profoundly mishandled the POW/MIA problem.

Definition of POW/MIA

The subject of POW/MIAs requires some definitions. After the Second Indochina War—popularly known as the Vietnam War, even though Thailand, Burma, Laos and Cambodia saw U.S. combat action—hundreds of POWs returned alive, notably in OPERATION HOMECOMING, which concluded in April, 1973.

Those who did not return home are classified by the Department of Defense into two categories: POW/MIA—that is, those for whom there is some documentation that they were captured but never repatriated and KIA/BNRs—that is, those believed to have been killed in action, but whose bodies were not recovered. For the latter, there is no evidence of their death except DOD's evaluation of the circumstances, even though no physical evidence of death may be available.

In April, 1973, DOD reported that 2,383 personnel were unaccounted for: 1,259 POW/MIAs, and 1,124 KIA/BNRs. This study assumes that both categories of the unaccounted for deserve review. Since 1973, DOD has announced the return of 280 sets of remains, diminishing the over-all number by that amount.

In addition, there could well be an equal number of military personnel missing in action from various U.S. covert actions during the war. Since DOD files on covert actions have not been opened, and the participants in such actions never publicly identified, this inquiry could not establish any number for covert POW/MIAs. However, public source books and interviews with participants suggest that the issue of covert operations adds a substantial, but unknown, dimension to the MIA question which has received no scrutiny.

Review of Live-Sighting Documents

In this inquiry, staff has reviewed hundreds of U.S. Government classified, declassified, and open-source documents. In addition, Senator Grassley and Committee Minority staff were given access to, and have reviewed personally, hundreds of classified live-sighting reports (accounts by Southeast Asians of live POWs in Southeast Asia) in the files of the Defense Intelligence Agency (DIA). According to DIA, this is the first time that either a United States Senator or any United States Congressional Committee staff have been given access to the raw intelligence contained in the 1,400 live-sighting reports.

Out of the 1,400 live-sighting reports, approximately 1,200 are considered by DIA to be "resolved." Each of the so-called "resolved" sightings was resolved by concluding that the live-sighting report did not pertain to U.S. POWs present after April 1979. Staff felt that in some cases such a conclusion was correct, but that in many it was not supported by the facts.

Staff began by first examining so-called resolved cases in order to study DIA methodology by which a conclusion of "resolution" was reached. Since the guidelines set by DIA for access to the files were extremely restrictive, the time available allowed review of only about one-quarter of the so-called "resolved" cases, and none of those in the category of "unresolved." Nevertheless, staff concluded that a significant number of the "resolved" cases reviewed showed that the DIA methodology was faulty, or that the evidence did not support the DIA conclusion in the case, or both.

The information collected and reviewed to date by the staff shows that the position held by the United States Government—namely, that no evidence exists that Americans are still being held against their will—cannot be supported. Rather, the information uncovered during this inquiry provides enough corroboration to cast doubt upon the veracity of the U.S. Government's conclusion.

Without revealing classified information, staff believes that the review of the classified live-sighting reports reinforces that doubt.

Although more information remains to be reviewed, the evidence this inquiry has thus far uncovered shows that:

1) living U.S. citizens, military and civilian were held in Southeast Asia against their will after the U.S. Government's statement on April 13, 1973, that no prisoners remained alive; and

2) the information available to the U.S. Government does not rule out the probability that U.S. citizens are still being held in Southeast Asia.

In fact, classified, declassified and unclassified information all confirm one startling fact: That DOD in April, 1974, concluded beyond a doubt that several hundred living American POWs remained in captivity in Southeast Asia. This was a full year after DOD spokesmen were saying publicly that no prisoners remained alive.

Evidence uncovered in the several hundred cases reviewed thus far clearly demonstrates that, in a disturbing number of cases, DOD made significant errors in drawing conclusions about live-sighting reports, the presumed deaths of individuals, or about individuals that were unaccounted for at the conclusion of the war. Although many cases were resolved correctly based upon the files, there were too many errors apparent to rule out the need to undertake and complete the review of the "unresolved" cases.

Staff also concluded that DOD spent an excessive amount of effort in discrediting live-sighting reports, while exaggerating or mishandling forensic data in order to confirm a presumptive finding of death. DOD appeared to be more anxious to declare a presumptive finding of death than in following up reports of sightings with creative investigative work.

Furthermore, there is evidence of insensitivity on the part of the Executive Branch of the U.S. Government in providing complete and accurate information to the next-of-kin of missing American servicemen.

The classified evidence in DIA files suggests a pattern by a few U.S. Government officials of misleading Congressional inquiries by concealing information, and misinterpreting or manipulating data in government files. Interested Senators and staff with proper clearances no doubt will want to review the classified files themselves and draw their own conclusions.

The 1973 Policy Decision

Those who have not dealt with the POW/MIA issue may find it difficult to understand how DOD's analysis of the information could be in error. Unfortunately, staff believes that DOD has allowed its procedures to be dictated by a pre-conceived policy finding.

The *New York Times* reported on April 12, 1973, as follows:

WASHINGTON, April 12 (AP)—The Pentagon, two months after the first American prisoners of war began coming home, said today that it had no evidence that there were any more prisoners still alive in all of Indochina.

Despite the fact that interviews with all returning prisoners are nearly complete, a Pentagon official, Dr. Roger Shields, said that none of the 1,389 Americans listed as missing were now technically considered prisoners. "We have no indication at this time that there are any Americans missing alive in Indochina," Dr. Shields said at a news conference.

Dr. Shields was at that time Assistant Secretary of Defense, but he was following guidance issued on that date by the Department of State in a memorandum to DOD which stated that "There are no more prisoners in Southeast Asia. They are all dead." This directive was issued immediately after the return of the last POWs in OPERATION HOMECOMING. This finding was made despite that the fact that none of the hundreds of POW/MIAs that the Pathet Lao publicly acknowledged holding were ever returned from Laos. There were hundreds of live-sighting reports on file in 1973. Thousands of such reports have continued to be received since then.

Process for "Presumption of Death"

Since it was official policy, then, that all MIAs were dead, it became a bureaucratic necessity for all "unresolved" cases to be resolved in favor of a presumed finding of death.

Each respective military service from time to time convenes its own special commissions to pronounce on individual cases. Such a commission has before it at least three categories of information: The first is intelligence-related information concerning the individual. The second is eyewitness accounts of the loss event. The third is the so-called "incident report"—the official report of the loss incident.

If a year passes without new information, the respective military service can convene a commission to determine whether a presumptive finding of death should be declared.

The April, 1973, statement of policy was a political statement, rather than a finding according to statutory authority. As a result, the military services subsequently reviewed each individual case of those who previously had been declared dead *en masse*. And in every case except one, the commissions made a determination of a presumptive finding of death.

Because of this procedure, the bureaucratic necessity arose for discrediting any evidence that might cast doubt on the mass presumptive finding of death of April, 1973. From the standpoint of law and military regulations, the procedure followed in each case gave a legal affirmation to the original political statement.

Therefore, in order to discredit any information which might undermine the political thesis, the analysis of intelligence files fell into a systematic pattern of debunking information contrary to the thesis.

This systematic debunking included discrediting reports, possible intimidation of witnesses, dismissal of credible evidence through technicalities, and—if all else failed—the arbitrary disregard of evidence contrary to the thesis.

DOD's Working Hypothesis

An analysis of DOD's working hypothesis for fully accounting for American MIAs is the key to understanding the discrepancies between DOD's position on the POW issue and the evidence uncovered by the staff.

DOD's premise, beginning in April, 1973, has been that all MIAs are dead; the corollary, therefore, is that DOD must never find any evidence that any MIA is alive. The best evidence, in DOD's opinion, is a set of physical remains that can be identified as a specific individual on the POW/MIA list. Once such an identification has been made, the case of that individual can be removed forever from the list. This is an easier task than to accept live-sighting reports that might point to a living POW, thereby necessitating appropriate follow-up action.

It is a reasonable assumption to remove POW/MIAs from the list when remains are identified, if the identification is correct. But the fact is that in a significant number of cases, such identifications have been made on the basis of inadequate physical evidence, using presumptive deductions that may or may not be true. The pressure to identify sets of remains even has resulted in specific cases where caskets have been buried with full military honors as the "remains" of the individual when, in fact, the casket is empty.

Therefore, DOD acts on its premise by vigorously investigating for the remains of dead MIAs. The list of MIAs presumed dead following the conclusion of the war totalled 2,383. DOD has received and claimed to have identified a total of 280 sets of remains since 1973.

Any full accounting of MIAs, according to DOD's working hypothesis, would necessarily involve only those cases in which either a presumptive finding of death could be made, or else full or partial remains could be discovered. As each presumptive finding of death is declared or set of remains is identified, DIA would remove, as accounted for, the names that matched those on the original MIA list. In this respect, DOD claims that DIA has vigorously investigated and resolved hundreds of such cases.

The policy of DOD is to focus attention on the cases where some evidence, no matter how small, of physical remains can be recovered. But even while DOD enthusiastically and vigorously investigates remains case—no matter how fragmentary—it just as vigorously discredits live-sighting and other witness accounts. Throughout the 1970s and 1980s hundreds of thousands of Asians fled Vietnam, Cambodia and Laos. These refugees provided many first-hand reports, or knew by second- or third-hand reports, of American prisoners being held in their respective countries.

To date, over 11,700 accounts have been received by DOD; 1,400 of these are first-hand, live-sighting reports. DIA claims to have analyzed fully each of these live-sighting reports, and to have left "no stone unturned" in searching for living prisoners. After analyzing the live-sighting reports, DIA has concluded that the majority are not related to living American POWs, with the possible exception of a small percentage of reports that DIA describes as "unresolved."

However, no "resolved" case has ever concluded that an American POW remains captive in Southeast Asia. In this way DIA concludes that there is no evidence of Americans currently being held captive in Southeast Asia. This contention is consistent with both the working hypothesis described above and with DIA's apparent success at removing from the MIA list names that involve only those cases in which remains are identified, or a finding of death declared.

Insofar as these discrepancies relate to the 1,400 first-hand reports of living prisoners, DOD's original premise comes into question. Numerous live-sighting reports have been erroneously discredited by DIA analysts. Moreover, staff has reason to believe that DOD has misidentified the remains of scores of MIAs, and has incorrectly presumed dead many others.

This analytical bias is typical of bureaucracy defending an established policy at all costs, even if it means denying the obvious. It is also a typical characteristic of an out-moded paradigm that can no longer explain the real world or real facts. If the original premise of DOD had been that at least *some* of the 2,383 MIAs were alive, then DOD would have been forced by circumstance to view the evidence collected, including the hundreds of live-sighting reports, from an objective standpoint. The relevance and validity of each report could have been judged on its own merits rather than whether it supported a pre-determined hypothesis that no living POW/MIAs remained.

Unfortunately, DOD choose to make its own analysis, without proper legislative oversight. Claiming extreme sensitivity and possible threats to sources and methods of intelligence gathering, DOD evaded the proper oversight that would have assured the objectivity of their progress. The result has been a disservice to the POW/MIAs, their families and the American people.

Importance of the Problem

The resolution of these questions is important not only to any MIA/POWs who may be still alive, but also the families involved. It is also important to the fate of any possible POWs in a future military action. With 200,000 U.S. troops now deployed to the Persian Gulf, the question of possible prisoners of war once again becomes an urgent matter.

Moreover, the resolution of issues relating to Southeast Asia is a key priority of our nation's foreign policy. Secretary of State James A. Baker III stated recently that the POW/MIA issue is the last remaining obstacle to resumption of relations with the government of Vietnam. But if it turns out that Vietnam has been concealing the evidence of POWs, then it would be a complicating factor in initiating relations with the present regime.

C

Addendum to the Oct. 29, 1990 Senate Report on the Southeast Asian POW/MIA Issue

Several weeks after they released the preceding report, the Senate investigators issued an eighty-two-page addendum to the Interim Report elaborating on four aspects of the POW/MIA issue: 1) live sighting reports; 2) presumptive findings of death and identification of remains; 3) "black," or covert operations; and 4) historical perspectives of the issue. The addendum also contained a section of historical background citing "precedents when the United States government, as a matter of policy, abandoned U.S. prisoners of war from other conflicts during the twentieth century, including World War I, World War II, and the Korean War. Using declassified U.S. government documents, including official cables, memos, and intelligence reports, a disturbing pattern was revealed which must be unsettling to those who reject, apriori, the concept that U.S. officials would ever abandon U.S. POWs."

The eighty-two-page addendum concluded by calling for a commitment by the entire Senate Foreign Relations Committee to determine who was responsible for the official decision to abandon some of the U.S. servicemen held prisoner at the end of the Vietnam War, as well as who is responsible for the failure to secure their release:

> To date, this inquiry has not established responsibility for the monumental decisions that have occurred affecting U.S. citizens held by adversary governments during the Second Indochina War. There is no question that a large number of U.S. citizens, military and civilian, as well as citizens from allied countries that aided United States efforts in Southeast Asia from 1955 through 1975, were taken captive by North Vietnam or the adversary movements engaged in warfare with the legitimate governments of the Republic of Vietnam, Laos, and Cambodia. It is apparent some of those known to have been captured by these forces died while in captivity, but the differences in the numbers returned and the numbers known to be prisoners, or those listed as missing are too great to go unchallenged. It can be assumed United States officials of the various departments knew a large number of U.S. citizens were being held captive; the negotiators of the Paris Peace Accords had to have this knowledge also; and the various administrations and their appointees must have known this information as well. Whatever the reasons are for keeping the secret, it has not resulted in the return of anyone, with the exception of Robert Garwood who found his own way out. There may be others like Garwood there yet and perhaps they only need some encouragement to find their way out too.

> In order to fix responsibility for the initial decisions to leave U.S. citizens captive, and establish who was responsible for maintaining that secret, it will be necessary to expand this inquiry beyond its present scope. This will require a commitment from the entire Committee. Increased funding and staffing combined with the investigative authority of the Senate will be necessary in order to fix responsibility for this problem.

D

Excerpts from the Statement of Tracy E. Usry, Special Investigator, Senate Foreign Relations Committee, Minority Staff,
Feb. 7, 1991

The focus of our inquiry has centered on the following questions:

1. Does the U.S. Government possess valid information concerning living POWs in Southeast Asia?

2. Has the U.S. Government failed to act on information concerning living POWs in Southeast Asia?

3. Has the U.S. Government acted improperly to intimidate, coerce or discredit sources which have valid information concerning living POWs in Southeast Asia?

I will address each of these questions separately. The first question: Does the U.S. Government possess valid information concerning living POWs in Southeast Asia? The staff position on this issue is YES.

Our Interim Report of October 1990 speaks for itself. Additionally, the United States chief negotiator during the Paris Peace talks, Mr. Henry Kissinger, in his memoirs on the Vietnam Peace Accords, *Years of Upheaval* (pg. 33 & 34) said, "The United States was aware of at least nineteen American POWs in North Vietnamese custody that were not accounted for by the Vietnamese. LTC (Ret) Stuart A. Herrington points out in his book *Peace With Honor?*, that as one of several U.S. Military intelligence officers assigned to work with the North Vietnamese and Peoples Republic of China representatives during the period 1973–75, he was responsible for the location and return of POW/MIAs believed to be held by the communists. According to Herrington, North Vietnamese officials stated that the failure to have all POW/MIAs returned was, because of the U.S. Government's failure to live up to the promise of four billion dollars in war reparations made to North Vietnam by President Nixon. The North Vietnamese position was: "U.S. casualties under North Vietnamese control would be accounted for and prisoners returned after fulfillment of the promise." The existence of live American POWs still in Southeast Asia during the period April 1973–75 was reinforced by our interviews with other American personnel assigned to Vietnam during the same time frame as Herrington. In addition, information developed during our inquiry shows the U.S. Government was aware of several Americans being held by North Vietnam who were considered collaborators, military deserters, or persons Absent Without Leave (AWOL) when captured by the North Vietnamese. The most prominent of this group was Mr. Robert Garwood, a former Marine, captured in DaNang in 1965 and released from Vietnam through his own efforts in 1979. Mr. Garwood, although court-martialed for collaboration with the enemy and striking/mistreating a prisoner, is living proof that the U.S. Government's position on living Americans in North Vietnam after 1973 is incorrect. Declassified Defense Intelligence Agency reports contained in the volumes of the *Uncorrelated Information Relating to*

Missing Americans in Southeast Asia, dated December 15, 1978, as well as declassified Central Intelligence Agency reports indicate that Garwood was tracked by U.S. Intelligence agencies from shortly after his capture in 1965 until his return in 1979.

* * *

The answer to the second question, "Has the U.S. Government failed to act on information concerning living POWs in Southeast Asia?" is YES. This is really a twofold problem. First is the analysis of live sighting reports by the Defense Intelligence Agency, second is the various procedures used by the U.S. Government to resolve cases of individuals missing as a result of the Southeast Asian War. The missing are accounted for through the process of declaring a person as Killed in Action/Body Not Recovered (KIA/BNR); a Presumptive Finding of Death is made; or the identification of partial remains by the Central Identification Laboratory–Hawaii, permanently closes a file.

The first issue is the greatest part of the problem. The Defense Intelligence Agency was a recipient of information collected on American POWs during the Vietnam War as well as after the war. The majority of the relevant information concerning live American POWs was during the time frame of 1960 through 1986. This is also the period in which the analysis of POW information from Southeast Asia was not always accurate. It appears from a review of a portion of the live-sighting reports, that Department of Defense analysts started with a premise that the information provided by non-American sources was a lie and then worked towards substantiating that premise as true. In some of the cases reviewed, where information would tend to substantiate a sighting as being accurate and that of a live POW, the information would be later disregarded. In one instance, a DIA analyst was asked why pertinent information was disregarded. His reply was that the source had recanted that portion of his statement. The problem was that the information on the source recanting that portion of his statement was nowhere in the file. It is quite apparent that the analysis

seemed bias toward establishing the source a liar, rather than attempting to substantiate the information provided by the source.
The vast majority of the intelligence collection efforts by the DIA,
as well as the Joint Casualty Resolution Center, were not professional in our judgement. As established by this inquiry, there was
a shortage of qualified personnel to collect POW intelligence, especially during the mass exodus of refugees from Southeast Asia following the 1975 fall of governments in Vietnam, Laos and
Cambodia. In essence, DOD has been able to construct a rationale
to discredit officially nearly every live-sighting report. In addition
to the example previously cited, the staff found instances where
the Defense Department merely excluded from its analysis certain
details of a valid sighting, such as a source's statement about the
number of POWs sighted, their physical condition, a description
of the camp or cave held in, whether they were shackled, or,
whether they were gesturing for food. By excluding such corrobo-
rating details, these details would not be known to anyone reading
just a summary of the report or DOD's analysis of the report. In
many instances in which a timely follow-up interview would have
expeditiously resolved a live-sighting report, there was a general
lack of emphasis on resolving the case within the system, and the
follow-up interviews did not occur for many months. Already
frightened refugees became confused by the failure of the U.S.
Government agents to accept their information.

*   *   *

The answer to the third question, "Has the U.S. Government
acted improperly to intimidate, coerce or discredit sources which
have valid information concerning live POWs in Southeast Asia?",
again, it is the staff's position that the answer is YES. I would now
like to cite some examples of this.

During the period 1984 through 1986, while serving as a Special Agent in the United States Army Criminal Investigation
Command, I was the Investigating Officer in which Maj. (Ret)

Mark Smith levied allegations against certain military officers stationed in Korea, who among other things failed to take appropriate action concerning information provided by him on possible live American POWs being held in Laos. During the course of this investigation, there was pressure placed on me by superiors to gather evidence discrediting Maj. Smith, rather than to pursue the allegations made by Smith. During the course of the investigation, and as a result of interviewing several people, I found that in one instance, Smith's source of information was deliberately compromised by members of the Defense Attache's Office in Thailand. The normal investigative process was not allowed to occur in order to prevent potential embarrassment to an Army general; statements were made concerning Smith's mission as the Commander of the Army Special Forces Unit in Korea, which omitted certain information, giving the impression that Maj. Smith was acting without authority in some areas; and his chances for promotion violated through the manipulation of the administrative process utilized for promotion. Somewhat after the fact, Smith's superiors did take steps to determine if Smith's information was valid; however, by that time Smith was so disgusted with the process that he ceased cooperating with the Army.

* * *

During the course of this investigation, the staff has seen at least four instances in which the Defense Intelligence Agency's reply to congressional inquiry has not been based totally in fact. In every instance, the omission of certain relevant information in the respective file would lead the reader to believe that there was no validity to the constituent's claim of unfair or less than professional handling of their problem by the Defense Intelligence Agency. In one instance, after reading DIA's response to a congressman's inquiry for POW/MIA related data, I commented to the DIA analyst that this letter, signed by Col. Joseph Schlatter, was not representative of the facts as they appear in the respective file. The

DIA analyst agreed with my comments and further stated that there were other instances of not actually presenting all the facts from a file similar to this one.

Thus far, I have given you examples of the three questions this inquiry has answered. In addition, I would like to address the issue of the Defense Department's lack of cooperation with Congressional inquiries on this subject. In one instance, at various times within a four month period, one Congressman and two Senators, separately, requested access to live sighting reports as well as other documents held by the Defense Intelligence Agency.

The Department of Defense took between two and four months to respond to their requests. Once the request was granted, in at least two instances the requirements for access were so restrictive as to make total access impossible. The Defense Department allowed access to the Live Sighting Reports only when a Senator was available to escort staff personnel to the Defense Intelligence Agency. Then, the Senator had to stay with the staff personnel at all times in order for access to continue. This requirement was not levied because of a clearance or access problem, as all staff personnel present had the appropriate clearances, rather, this requirement was meant to hinder the review process.

This requirement is totally out of line in regards to how the Defense Department works internally. It is routine for staff personnel in the Defense Department to do the research, then provide the pertinent facts to the superior. This then allows the superior to do his work while the staff does the research. Apparently, the Defense Department didn't feel that a Senator's time was equally as important as that of their own senior officers. The matter of access to the additional documents requested, both the Tighe Commission Report as well as the Gains Report (an in-house evaluation of the effectiveness of the DIA POW/MIA section, done by one of the previous Chiefs of the section) have still not been addressed satisfactorily by the Defense Department.

In yet another instance, a request for information was made through the Defense Department's Office of Congressional Liaison, which took over two months to be acted on, before a reply was forthcoming. It would seem that the Defense Department places little or no priority on responding to requests concerning this sensitive issue. This seems rather strange, when the majority of those still missing were members of the same department.

I addressed the issue earlier in this statement that the Staff reviewed the U.S. Government's position concerning POW/MIAs from previous wars. The period reviewed was from 1917 through the Korean War. Based on the documentation reviewed by the Staff, it is apparent that American POWs as well as allied POWs were left unaccounted for after World War II and Korea. In both instances, prisoners were taken by the Soviets and never returned. Not only did the Soviets keep American and Allied prisoners liberated from German prison camps, they continued to kidnap American soldiers off the streets of Europe. At the end of the Korean conflict, American and allied prisoners were kept by the North Koreans, Peoples Republic of China as well as the Soviets. The numbers reflected as being kept by the various communist governments exceeds eighty thousand.

I would like to close with a quote from a document published by the National League of Families, titled *Conspiracy and Coverup*, dated October 1988,

> Those long involved are acutely aware that information was distorted or withheld in years past; however, now is *not* the time for those who are currently working this issue to undertake an historical investigation of past efforts—history will take care of itself. The league holds the firm conviction that efforts must focus on the present and future. Our men's lives may well depend on current decisions; they do not depend on history except in the context of policy negotiations.

I would submit that the real problem with the POW problem is historical. It is the intelligence information of the past that was poorly handled, analyzed with a bias of disproving the information, the past identifications of remains though inaccurate, or as what some people believe to be fraudulent means, as well as the past discretion of the Defense Department to discredit people providing what they knew or believed to be valid information.

It is the Defense Department's past handling of the issue in general, as well as a basic mistrust of the Defense Intelligence Agency's ability to properly analyze information, which has ceased the flow of valuable information concerning the possibility of live Americans still being held in foreign countries around the world. Unless the past history is corrected, this issue will never be resolved.

Index